Forming: The Early Days of L.A. Punk
Track 16 Gallery: 10 April–5 June, 1999

Track 16 Gallery / Smart Art Press
Bergamot Station
2525 Michigan Avenue, Building C1
Santa Monica, California 90404
310-264-4678 (tel)
310-264-4682 (fax)
www.smartartpress.com

Smart Art Press
Volume VI, No. 57 Second Edition

© 1999, 2000 Smart Art Press

All rights reserved. No part of this publication may be reproduced, stored in a retrieval system, or transmitted in any form or by any means, electronic, mechanical, photocopying, recording, or otherwise, without prior written permission of Smart Art Press.

Cover: Tomata Du Plenty, ca. 1977. Melanie Nissen.
Frontispiece and back cover: Circle Jerks crowd (detail), ca. 1980. Ann Summa.

All photographs and images © 1999 the artists

Essays © 1999 the authors

Exhibition curators / catalogue editors: Exene Cervenka, Susan Martin, Kristine McKenna, Holly Myers, Pilar Perez, Viggo Mortensen, John Roecker
Design: Steve Samiof and Mick Haggerty, Brains
Copy Editing: Sherri Schottlaender

Distributed by DAP
155 Avenue of the Americas
New York, New York 10013
1-800-338-BOOK

ISBN 1-889195-44-8

Printed in Spain, Jomagar, S.L.

Dedicated to Claude Bessy

FORMING: THE EARLY DAYS OF L.A. PUNK

essays
Claude Bessy
Chris Morris
Kristine McKenna
Sean Carrillo
Exene Cervenka and John Doe

photographers
Edward Colver
Diane Gamboa
Frank Gargani
Jenny Lens
Gary Leonard
Jonathan Louie
Melanie Nissen
Donna Santisi
Ann Summa

SMART ART PRESS

Claude Bessy, aka Kickboy Face, at *Slash* headquarters, ca. 1979. Ann Summa.

KICKBOY FACE EXPLAINS IT ALL FOR YOU

Any historical moment worth its salt has its resident scribe, and during the 1970s Los Angeles had Claude Bessy. Writing under the pen name Kickboy Face, Bessy was the star reporter at *Slash* magazine from 1977 until October of 1980 when he decided he'd had enough of America and decamped to London. (Bessy presently lives in Barcelona.)

For four glorious years, however, Bessy covered the L.A. waterfront. Accompanied by his indefatigable companion Philomena (who made the Bessy reign of anarchy possible by loving him and looking after him), Bessy was everywhere at once. A transplanted Frenchman with an astonishing capacity for mood-altering chemicals, he seemed to miss nothing, and he functioned as the punk community's conscience and head cheerleader. He also wrote like an angel. Rooted in a searing disgust for the general mediocrity of the human race which was worthy of Céline, Bessy's writing combined a messianic belief in the redemptive power of music with a scrupulous honesty. As can be seen in the following excerpts, no one was spared when Kickboy sat down to write. Herewith, a few of his greatest hits.

—Kristine McKenna

```
     OPENING SALVO (May '77): "Lately there've been rumors of
strange goings-on in the music world. Violence at concerts, out-
raged editorials in newspapers, foul-mouthed interviews on TV,
frightened record company executives, oddball fashions, repulsive
makeup, and dirty, primitive music that has little to do with the
stuff the music industry has been pouring into our ears for an
eternity.
     "This publication was born out of hope regarding the rebirth
of true rebel music and its eventual victory over the bland product
professional pop stars have been feeding us. May the punks set this
rat-infested industry on fire. It sure could use a little bright-
ness!"
```

THE SEX PISTOLS' FIRST SINGLE (May '77): "The sweet sound of chaos. Johnny Rotten sneering and spitting his absolute refusal of anything that is anything. One long fuzzy overloaded riff that is the greatest rejection of studio rock since god knows when. It's not enough to be aware of the fact that the rock we hear on the radio is zombie food for idiots in nowhereland, background music for young executives on their swinging little weekend gettogethers. Fuck the clean licks at the perfect time, fuck the clever rhythms, fuck the vocal harmonies. Thank the Pistols for one of the most important rock singles since 'Satisfaction.'"

THE CLASH (August '77): "Like fourteen hand grenades tossed down the pants of the music world, The Clash's first LP is here. There is so much fire, rawness, economy and brilliance here that it makes just about everything else obsolete. Just a few seconds listening to the first cut and you're right there in the middle of their world, where crushed dreams are the rule. I haven't recovered from this album yet. Some of you won't either."

CHELSEA (September '77): "Gene October looks real angry in the picture on the sleeve of this single. I'm not sure I'll go along with him on the 'right to work' bit 'cause I'm a lazy bastard myself and I can't get too worked up about being unable to spend five days a week in a factory. But then again, I don't know what it's like being a futureless kid in Britain, so I'll stop being cute and irrelevant."

ELVIS COSTELLO'S DEBUT LP (October '77): "Don't know why I bought this one because Elvis don't look too heavy on the cover. I must've been drunk that day. Actually the music is much worse than the cover; it's fucking boring shit that was boring already three years ago. It's music to smoke joints to while the dogs are playing on the rug and the old lady is making her famous stew in her earth-catalogue kitchen with the racks full of spices and the herb charts on the wall. I couldn't swear, but I believe they even use a fuckin' dobro."

    EDITORIAL (February '78): "All right children, let's get a few things straight. There ain't no *Slash* philosophy and there ain't no *Slash* T-shirts. If we rounded up the multitude of misfits who write, doodle and punch noses for our cause in the same room it would lead to a full-scale rumble. How could we offer a united philosophical front under such conditions? Which means that you, too, with the Roxy Music hangover, can write for *Slash*, as long as you've reformed and are humbly willing to start a new, meaningful life.

    "Narrow-minded as we are, we are vaguely aware there are other things in life besides punk. There are Kiss, Rick Wakeman, and Idi Amin. There's probably more. When we do not review your band or publish your poetry it is by no means a sign of disapproval. We are simply completely uninterested. Others may not be. Good luck.

    "Music cannot stand still and experimentation is vital. Some of you have even discovered that if you take chances you get a different sound. Keep at it. You'll soon find that the ways to get all those burning, formless urges across are countless."

    THE ZIPPERS (February '78): "If you expect me to slag this just on principle, fuck you. The Zippers are good at what they do and though it's not my fave type of noise, that's not their problem. Excuse me, Zippers, while I tiptoe out to the alley to do some intensive sipping with the rest of the spikey degenerates. Nothing personal."

I got brain cells to spare, try anything once

MARY MONDAY SINGLE (February '78): "I like this song, much to my surprise. It cooks real modern, no fooling around, too bad for the solo that almost drives the song into oblivion. Bad judgment there. That guitar player should've been briefed on the wonders of economy. Five seconds would've been quite enough for him to flash and go, 'Hey, mom, look, I'm recording a fucking solo!'"

PATTI SMITH IN REDONDO BEACH (April '78): "We pay two dollars, which is cool considering that we're about to see 'the first lady of punk rock.' And it starts. Patti does not know what the fuck she is about anymore. A poetess is the last thing this generation wants, but Patti has made up her mind to lay some culture on the kids. There is some interesting heckling. The show then became a rock'n'roll jam session, after which Miss Inspiration walked off surrounded by admirers. Someone handed her a *Slash*, which she threw on the floor. The star had bigger things on her mind. Three days later I got to see some naked pics of Patti in [a] leather outfit when she didn't think she was chosen by the gods to carry The Word. She's got better tits than I thought, though."

THE ELECTRIC CHAIRS SINGLE (April '78): "Wayne just won't quit. This time we get the touching story of Eddie and Sheena who, in spite of peer pressure, get married and name their brat Elvis Rotten. I'm not making this up. Maybe Wayne will stop his novelty record business after he makes enough for that costly sex change."

HARRY TOLEDO AND THE ROCKETS EP (April '78): "Another proof of the odd lucidity of the truly insane. Mr. Toledo may not be a loony himself, but his music belongs in the 'padded cell rock' category. The various elements are rather innocent when taken separately, but when everything meets it simply becomes deranged. I ain't saying even one or two persons might go for this EP, and I don't want no complaints afterwards about my lack of taste. If you wanna be safe buy the collected works of 999. Me, I don't care. I got brain cells to spare. I'll try anything once."

VOM AT THE WHISKEY (May '78): "I may be stupid, but I still haven't figured out what Richard Meltzer and company are trying to do. They couldn't have jumped on a bandwagon they so obviously loathe out of sheer boredom. They couldn't be stupid enough to believe their 'infiltration' could discredit a movement that doesn't have much credit to start with. They couldn't be naive enough to think that even on the fringe of this fringe phenomenon there's room for a bunch of would-be satirists with bitterness in their hearts and potbellies behind their stage costumes. Why the fuck did they choose punk as the target of their combined 'wit'? The punx know how to make fun of themselves much better, so where does that leave Vom?"

PLASTIC BERTRAND SINGLE (May '78): "Factory-made 'new' music for continental kiddies who find the real new sound hard to swallow. Studio musicians, sound gimmicks, singing puppets just like they love them on European variety shows. There's even a Beach Boys cliche to make sure absolutely everyone gets their money's worth. They're eating it up in France. Disco punk. It had to happen."

THE NORMAL (July '78): "Another possible 'next big thing?' Techno-pop for tomorrow's teenaged robots? Both songs are 80% rhythm machine, 10% emotionless spoken delivery and 10% modern-society

Exene Cervenka and Claude conspire, ca. 1977. Melanie Nissen.

evocations. Does this mean that every loony and would-be artist that the punk thing left behind will rush into the studio and single-handedly produce a bleak little single? 'Just me and my machines, man, I don't need nothing else . . .'"

SHAM 69 LP (July '78): "Some people are in punk rock 'cos it's the cool thing to do. Some are in it 'cos they think it's the best way to attract attention. Jimmy Pursey and the boys don't have a choice. It's either that or the bloody factory. Either grab a mike or a guitar, or work for the bosses for the rest of your grey life. No matter if the sound you come up with ain't exactly sophistico, you make up for it by sheer conviction and honesty. The live side may make some wince with its simplistic thump thump feel and its barbaric chants between songs, but it's obviously the most representative of Sham's style: basic rock'n'roll that all the angry kids in the filthy city can beat the shit out of each other to. There isn't much point in separating the songs—it's one long explosion of frustration. Listen to the audience shouting itself hoarse; when all hell breaks loose in the industrial world, this is what the mob will sound like."

THE OTHERS AT THE OTHER MASQUE (March '79): "The Others sounded like every other band but played longer than most. They could've been vaguely promising two years ago, but a lot of safety pins have gone under the bridge since then. They even look kind of angry but by now only the lettuce at Safeway don't look angry. It's O.K. music to drink beer to, but somebody minded and pulled the plug on them. Big hassle, the girl singer insults Brendan (so what's new?), they scream bloody rip-off, but the 22 people in the audience couldn't care less."

THE SUBURBAN LAWNS (March '79): "The Suburban Lawns aren't bad, but when Miss Su Tissue joined them for three songs there suddenly was the feeling of an unusual event taking place. The intensity of her neurotic performance, her quivering, clenched attempts at grasping the microphone stand, the deformed shape of her face while she spews out her lyrics—it was all slightly awesome. That strange, unfashionably dressed girl (a long, shapeless dress gathered in a gruesome oversized balloon at the waist with matching headband!) sang like others slip into the first stage of an epileptic fit. Absolutely unlike anybody else in the vocal originality sweepstakes."

THE OFFS (May '79): "Screw the reggae purists, this is all right. Recorded inside a corrugated tin shack, it jumps real good. I'm gonna get myself a pint of rum and blast it 'til something happens."

JOHNNY COUGAR EP (May '79): "Place this at the top of the pile of records that have no reason to exist; four plodding rock shit tunes that will remain a gaping nothing way after the end of the universe."

THE FALL LP (May '79): "This is more than a step forward — it's a giant leap and is possibly no longer punk as we know it. This is music and words for insomniacs with a chip on their shoulder, music for kids with nothing to lose and for musicians with everything to learn. This is ruthless teen genius music for a real better future and Devo are just reactionary comedians with a linear brain pattern. This album is altering my genes better than the Harrisburg evening winds."

THE FLYBOYS SINGLE (August '79): "The Flyboys think we don't like them 'cos they're pop punk. Well, they're full of it. And why should it matter whether we like something or not, I mean, we're not exactly in a position where we mold public taste. We thought Van Halen was a joke, but who's laughing now? We're just a pack of off-the-wall weirdos with fringe leanings. Everybody knows that, so what's all the fuss over our monthly bitchy verdicts?"

LOCAL OPERATOR SINGLE (October '79): "Immoral waste of a catchy Caribbean backbeat on A side. These guys are straining so hard to be 'infectious' they're gonna pop a hemorrhoid. Gruesome bizness, pop music."

X (August '79); "Everything has been said. Everything is true. They are the greatest, the best, the baddest, the whole L.A. enchilada by themselves. Every note, every riff, every wail is a microcosm of everything we've ever believed in, danced to and prayed for."

This is music and words for insomniacs with a chip on their shoulder

L.A. PUNK BY CHRIS MORRIS

"The bearers of the myth of every decade seem to carry in their hands the ax and the spade to execute and inter the myth of the previous one," journalist Murray Kempton wrote in *Part of Our Time: Some Ruins and Monuments of the Thirties* (1955). Kempton was describing how American communists and radicals of the thirties swept aside the extravagance and frivolity of the Roaring Twenties, but he probably would have been able to detect a similar impulse in the punk-rock jihad that rose up in Los Angeles in the late seventies.

The generational-cultural conflict explicit in punk was stated succinctly in the full-page cartoon *Pretty Vacant*, signed by "Blotch," in the back pages of *Slash #1*, in which a punk daydreams about burying a knife deep in the back of a peace-sign–flashing hippie.

When punk rock detonated for real in L.A. in 1977, it was making a somewhat belated arrival. The first wave of American punks—Patti Smith, Television, Richard Hell & the Voidoids, the Ramones—had been active in New York from 1974 on (as had such proto-punk Cleveland bands as the Electric Eels, Mirrors, and Rocket from the Tombs), and members of the group that became the Sex Pistols began to coalesce in 1975 around the Kings Road shop of the Machiavellian London entrepreneur Malcolm McLaren, who had cocked an early eye toward the New York scene.

To be sure, the tardiness of the punk upheaval here may have had something to do with the fact that L.A. has always been a music-biz company town resistant to change and hardly susceptible to revolt. However, by 1977 the disenchanted youth of L.A. found that there was a little too much to rebel against for them to sit still any longer.

It was post-Watergate, post-Viet Nam, post-Bicentennial; America had elected a peanut farmer as president. Disco held sway atop the charts: the number-one hits of 1976 included Wild Cherry's "Play that Funky Music," KC & the Sunshine Band's

"(Shake, Shake, Shake) Shake Your Booty," and the Bee Gees' "You Should Be Dancing." The following year, the latter group of retreaded Swinging London antiques would cement their renascent stardom with the *Saturday Night Fever* soundtrack, the source of every lumpen hustler's white-bread disco fantasy. The top hit of 1977 was Debby Boone's "You Light Up My Life." The biggest groups of the moment were L.A.–based: the Eagles, who struck platinum with the ultimate Southern California cocaine-cowboy exegesis *Hotel California*, and British transplants Fleetwood Mac, who followed up their massive self-titled 1975 album (their first with Angeleno musicians Lindsey Buckingham and Stevie Nicks) with the even more massive 1977 soft-pop behemoth *Rumours*.

While mass-culture oppression had clearly reached insupportable heights, the L.A. punks didn't really begin to pour out of the woodwork until the Sex Pistols, the Damned, and other U.K. bands arrived to sell American punk rock back to the Yanks. Though not without its fans, New York punk fell largely on deaf ears here; in L.A., pop culture has always played best with an English accent, and in the mid-seventies the city was very much a glam town where Brit rock stars were demigods and David Bowie reigned supreme. Some of the early L.A. punks were only recently reconstructed glamsters. Look at the history of the Germs, one of the first groups on the scene: singer Darby Crash—who, friends say, kept a virtual shrine to Bowie in his bedroom—and guitarist Pat Smear—who sometimes called himself Pat Bulsara in homage to Queen's Freddie Mercury, né Frederick Bulsara—met their future bandmates Belinda Carlisle and Lorna Doom in the lobby of the Beverly Hilton, where they were all lying in wait for Mercury.

Brendan Mullen, the irascible Scot who founded the Masque as L.A. punk's first full-time performance space, tartly encapsulated the push-and-pull between appropriated British grit and sun-soaked leisure-time trend-mongering on the L.A. scene in a December 1977 *Slash* ad for the club, which he

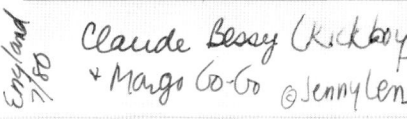

described as "a spectacle of simulated London street desperation in the promised land filtered through a rock-and-roll sensibility of carbonated freeway fury and terminal swimming-pool despair."

The rhetoric of *Slash* editor Claude Bessy—the hectoring theoretician and seriocomic conscience of L.A. punk—notwithstanding, most of the first L.A. punk bands were engaged in the music to foment, in Robinson Jeffers's still-useful term, revolution for the hell of it. They truly became revolutionaries only insofar as the music they were making was almost immediately rejected by the commercial establishment and had to be transmitted on do-it-yourself terms.

It was never easy for outsiders to score gigs or gain attention in L.A.: witness the pre-punk musical collective Radio Free Hollywood (the Motels, the Pop!, the Dogs), who mounted their own club dates and even published their own magazine. However, by the summer of 1977 the first L.A. punk groups—the Weirdos, the Screamers, the Germs, and San Diego transplants the Zeros—had played a handful of self-promoted shows at Hollywood's S.I.R. Studios and the Orpheum Theatre, a tiny room across the street from Tower Records on the Sunset Strip.

All the forces that would coalesce to make the underground scene visible and viable came to the fore almost simultaneously that season. Publishers Steve Samiof and Melanie Nissen and editor Bessy and his significant other Philomena published the first *Slash* in May; the fifty-cent rag quickly became local punk's bully pulpit, house organ, and gossip tabloid. In July—a month after Kim Fowley showcased the Zeros, the Weirdos, the Germs, the Screamers, and the Dils at his "New Wave Music" shows at the Whisky A Go Go— Mullen opened the Masque as a rehearsal space and low-priced music venue in a dank, grafitti-scarred basement behind the Pussycat porn theater on Hollywood Boulevard. And Rodney Bingenheimer (a Fowley cohort who formerly operated the Sunset Strip glam den Rodney's English Disco) was showcasing the new English

Rodney Bingenheimer, dubbed the mayor of the Sunset Strip by Sal Mineo, ca. 1978. Ann Summa.

Jan Paul Beahm, aka Bobby Pyn, aka Darby Crash, in stitches, ca. 1978. Jenny Lens

John Denny (Weirdos) with a fan at the Orpheum, ca. 1977. Jenny Lens.

groups—and later played the L.A. punkers—on his Sunday night show on the maverick Pasadena FM station KROQ.

It was admittedly a small scene which, thanks to the exposure it garnered from these significant outlets, appeared to be larger than it was. "*Slash* started as a bluff," Bessy told English writer Jon Savage in 1992. "We were pretending there was an L.A. scene when there was no scene whatsoever. The magazine was it. . . Then all these disaffected loonies started focusing on the mag and decided, 'We can be it, too.'"

The effect proved to be explosive. By late 1977 a host of bands had played at the Masque and had their pictures splattered across the pages of *Slash*. Though superficially alike in their economy and high velocity, the groups couldn't have been more dissimilar: the hypertense, keyboard-propelled, and sadly unrecorded Screamers (whose stark electroshocked logo by *Slash* cartoonist Gary Panter became L.A. punk's first recognizable icon); the spasmodic, trash-bag–bedecked Weirdos; the blatantly amateurish Germs, who nonetheless acquired a sizable cult thanks to the zit-encrusted charisma and dizzying lyrical talent of their self-destructing singer Darby Crash; the amphetamine-driven power trio the Alley Cats; political pogoers the Dils; the wailing Bags (so named because they initially performed with grocery sacks on their heads); the mocking, goofy gutter-punks Black Randy & the Metrosquad; X, which mated the angular vocals of Exene and John Doe to poetical noir candids of the L.A. streets; the jazz-brat Deadbeats, founded by the teenaged sons of top session drummer John Guerin, authors of the early anthem "Kill the Hippies"; stoopid-punk clowns Fear; and the shambolic all-non-star Arthur J. & the Gold Cups, named for a pair of sleazy Hollywood eateries and described by sometime-member Mullen as "a fuck-off party band."

The scene was comfortable in its diversity. Women took leading roles in defining the music's public face: Exene, the Alley Cats' Dianne Chai, the Bags' Alice and Pat Bag, the Eyes' Charlotte Caffey (who later co-led the all-girl Go-Go's, fronted by ex-Germ Belinda Carlisle), the Germs' Lorna Doom, the Controllers' Carla Mad Dog (a black woman, and one of the fiercest drummers in town), and later, Nervous Gender's Phranc and 45 Grave's Dinah Cancer were among the most prominent players. Latinos were also welcome: such pioneering players as the Plugz (led by Tito Larriva, who also ran his own label) and the Zeros were succeeded by East L.A. transplants like the Brat and Los Illegals. (The Latino roots

Belinda Carlisle (Go Go's), ca. 1981. Ann Summa.

Mary Grave, aka Dinah Cancer (45 Grave), ca. 1981. Ann Summa.

Exene, ca. 1981. Frank Gargani.

group Los Lobos, pelted with refuse when they opened a 1980 show for Public Image Ltd. at the Olympic Auditorium, became a reigning club attraction and, thanks to their "La Bamba" remake, a platinum act in the post-punk eighties.)

It was a frenetic and creative time, but major labels saw no marketability in the L.A. punk bands: who, after all, could find commercial value in pointed songs like "Destroy All Music," "I Hate the Rich," "We're Desperate," "Nothing Means Nothing Anymore," or "Manimal"? The majors opted instead to pluck groups from the host of relatively inoffensive "skinny-tie" pop bands (like the infamous Knack, L.A.'s big hit-makers of '79) which rose concurrently in the more legit L.A. clubs. Of the class of '77, only the unthreatening, chimplike Dickies were initially rewarded with a recording contract (from A&M, no less). X's claim in the song "The Unheard Music" that punk was "locked out of the public eye" could not have been more accurate.

Taking a cue from English (naturally) indie labels like Stiff and bands like the Buzzcocks, whose 1977 EP *Spiral Scratch* was the first homemade British punk 45, L.A. punks, by sheer necessity, took the D.I.Y. aesthetic to heart in the years 1977 to 1979. Chris Ashford, a clerk at Peaches Records on L.A.'s Westside, immortalized the Germs on the What? Records single "Forming"; Greg Shaw's Bomp, a spinoff of the like-named magazine, issued early records by the Zeros and the South Bay pop-punk unit the Last; *Slash* writer Chris Desjardins released the important compilation *Tooth and Nail* and an EP by his own band, the Flesh Eaters; the Plugz put out their own album, *Electrify Me* (Larriva's home phone number was carved into the runoff groove); and ex-Screamers keyboardist David Brown's Dangerhouse Records dropped a quick succession of seminal singles by X, the Weirdos, the Dils, the Alley Cats, the Deadbeats, and Black Randy, as well as the anthology *Yes L.A.* (an answer record of sorts to the 1978 "no wave" compilation *No New York*) and Black Randy's album, the elegantly titled *Pass the Dust, I Think I'm Bowie*. Even *Slash* got into the act: the magazine's own imprint issued Plugz and Germs singles, the Germs' sole album, *(GI)*, and in April 1980, X's long-awaited debut album, *Los Angeles*.

The first Black Flag EP, cover by Raymond Pettibon, ca. 1978. Collection of John Roecker.

Henry Rollins, the last of the Black Flag si

1981. Ann Summa.

By 1979 local punk's profile had risen considerably, albeit not very positively, as far as some pundits and city fathers were concerned, and new elements began to make the music a problematic quantity even for some of its early supporters. While a series of benefits for the Masque in February 1978, featuring virtually all of L.A. punk's early luminaries, had put the music on the map locally, the club had folded for good that year after Mullen unsuccessfully moved it to a location at Santa Monica and Vine. Though West Hollywood spots like the Whisky and the Starwood sporadically hired the groups, club managers mainly viewed punk as a headache, and the music ultimately flourished in far-flung dives like the Hong Kong Cafe in Chinatown, Blackie's in Hollywood, Al's Bar downtown, the Vex in East L.A., and Club 88 on the Westside. Occasionally a foolhardy promoter would mount a high-profile concert; one such show, earmarked for a live recording, effectively spelled the beginning of the end of Hollywood's punk Old Guard and ushered in an epoch in which L.A. punk was increasingly identified with public violence.

On March 17, 1979—St. Patrick's Day—a concert featuring X, the Alley Cats, the Bags, the Zeros, the Go-Go's, the Plugz, and Seattle's Wipers was mounted at the Elks Lodge Hall (the Park Plaza Hotel) near MacArthur Park. During the show, without provocation a platoon from the Los Angeles Police Department's Rampart Division invaded the hall in full riot gear and bloodily beat kids down the Park Plaza's steep staircase and up the street in a nightmare replay of the Odessa Steps sequence of Eisenstein's *Potemkin*.

Three months later a Hermosa Beach band called Black Flag issued its debut EP *Nervous Breakdown* on its own label, SST Records. This was the opening salvo of Southern California hardcore punk, an aggressive, speeded-up new genre that spoke to the malaise of monied yet disenchanted male teens who lived on the beachfronts south of L.A. In an April 1980 *Slash* review of a Black Flag show at the group's Redondo Beach stronghold, the Fleetwood, Bessy found the new strain an improbable development: "The beach bleached blond brats into punk? Come on! Even the blacks going punk was easier to imagine." But he added that the wound-up music was "most likely the first meaningful and useful thing these kids got their hands on since they were born. Yep, Sid lives all right, and now he's got himself a tan." The reference to the Sex Pistols' figurehead of senseless violence, bassist Sid Vicious (who died from a heroin overdose in October 1978 after being jailed for murdering his girlfriend), would prove chillingly apt.

From 1979 to 1981, the influence of Black Flag spawned a vital new round of independent recording by labels like SST, Posh Boy, Frontier, and New Alliance (run by San Pedro's politicized punk-funk trio the Minutemen, who stood somewhat apart from their hardcore brethren) and the rise of a slew of hardcore bands from the South Bay and Orange County: the Circle Jerks (fronted by Black Flag's original lead singer, Keith Morris), the Adolescents, the Descendents, the Crowd, Social Distortion, Agent Orange, T.S.O.L., China White. But the bands had a following of unpredictable and volatile young fans whose full-contact "dance" style—which produced the first mosh pits and the media-manufactured term "slamdancing"—was reflective of an abiding pugnacity. When the hardcore groups played Hollywood shows, they often became pitched battles, both in the clubs (where spectators might get gang-stomped by skinheaded fans for having unmodishly long hair) and in the streets (after nightstick-wielding cops descended on gigs at the Whisky, Baces Hall, Polish Hall, the Palladium, and other unlucky venues).

What we think of today as "L.A. punk rock" had atomized by 1982. Under law-enforcement fire, the beach-punk bands largely disappeared from L.A. venues. Black Flag, whose 1981 debut album *Damaged* was withdrawn by its major-label distributor, MCA, for its perceived "anti-parent" sentiments, took its hardcore gospel on the road with a virtually perpetual cycle of U.S. and foreign touring. Many of the original L.A. punk bands either soldiered on or disappeared entirely; Darby Crash's overdose suicide in December 1980 had signalled the end of an era. The old-school bands' followers who, in Brendan Mullen's piquant phrase, "flopped the hardcore testo rage rite," moved along to such musical diversions as post-punk roots-rock or the neopsychedelic "Paisley Underground." Some of the first-generation groups finally found homes at major labels: Wall of Voodoo, I.R.S., 1981; X, Elektra, 1982; the Alley Cats, MCA, 1982. X alone maintained its high artistic standards over a course of albums and is viewed today as the most significant and enduring act of the time.

Trudie, ca. 1978. Melanie Nissen.

Finally, in a development viewed with either horror or jaundiced amusement by those who knew them when, the Go-Go's, viewed as little more than an in-crowd gag in 1978, fired their original rhythm section, signed with I.R.S., and released a 1981 album, *Beauty and the Beat*, which spawned two top-twenty hit singles and sold two million copies. In this strange and ironic denouement, L.A. punk rock had become part and parcel of what it had innocently set out to demolish just four short years before.

Native habitat
(Coco's Club, downtown L.A.),
ca. 1982. Edward Colver.

It's comforting to remember that somewhere, at any given point in time, there's a cluster of people shaking their fists at society and screaming "fuck you." The dates, places, and guilty parties may change, but the sentiment burns on, shining and immutable. In the mid-seventies, one of those clusters coalesced in Los Angeles with the city's first flowering of punk rock.

Given a cursory glance, L.A. punk seemed to appear out of nowhere, apropos of nothing, but the territory had been mined sixty years before in Zurich, Switzerland, when Romanian poet Tristan Tzara, German writer Hugo Ball, and Alsatian artist Jean Arp came together to form the dadaists. Dedicated to opposing the aesthetic and social values then shaping human life, dada philosophy took root at approximately the same time in New York, where a similar revolution led by Marcel Duchamp, Man Ray, and Francis Picabia was taking place, and in Paris, where it morphed into surrealism under the tutelage of the tyrannical André Breton.

Remembrance of Things Fast by Kristine McKenna

Among the sentiments shared by these far-flung co-conspirators was a disdain for the mannered perversions of high art. Repressing the primal drives the dadaists revered, the bourgeois art of the Academy had allowed the public to drift off to sleep. The dadaists were out to wake people up, and towards that end they devised a methodology that was irreverent, difficult to comprehend, and deliberately shocking. Central to all their work was a belief in destruction as a creative act, a rejection of high culture, and an abhorrence for anything smacking of "good taste."

To be aggressively assaulted by something bewildering always has a quality of newness about it; this experience, however, came to be one of the enduring traditions of our century. From dada to surrealism to COBRA to Japan's Gutai collective to Fluxus to the Lettrist International to happenings to performance art to the Situationists, the twentieth century has always had a bloodless revolution of ideas occurring somewhere. As can be seen in several photographs included here, a bit of blood was shed on behalf of L.A.'s punk insurrection, but in keeping with the rules of dada, it was essentially a war of ideas.

Punk was an international movement, but it's generally agreed that it had three capital cities: London, New York, and Los Angeles. In purely visual terms, it manifested differently in each of them.

The look of British punk, for instance, was dominated by the ripped, "ransom note" graphic style developed by Jamie Reid, an artist loosely associated with the Situationists. A radical European art collective founded in the early fifties, the Situationists were committed to pitching the world into a state of constant revolution and newness. They obviously failed to achieve that goal, but they did leave a mark on punk in the form of impresario

Johanna Went in performance, ca. 1978. Frank Gargani.

Jimbo, by Gary Panter, from *Slash*, ca. 1979. Collection of John Roecker.

Flyer by Michael Uhlenkott, ca. 1980. Collection of John Roecker.

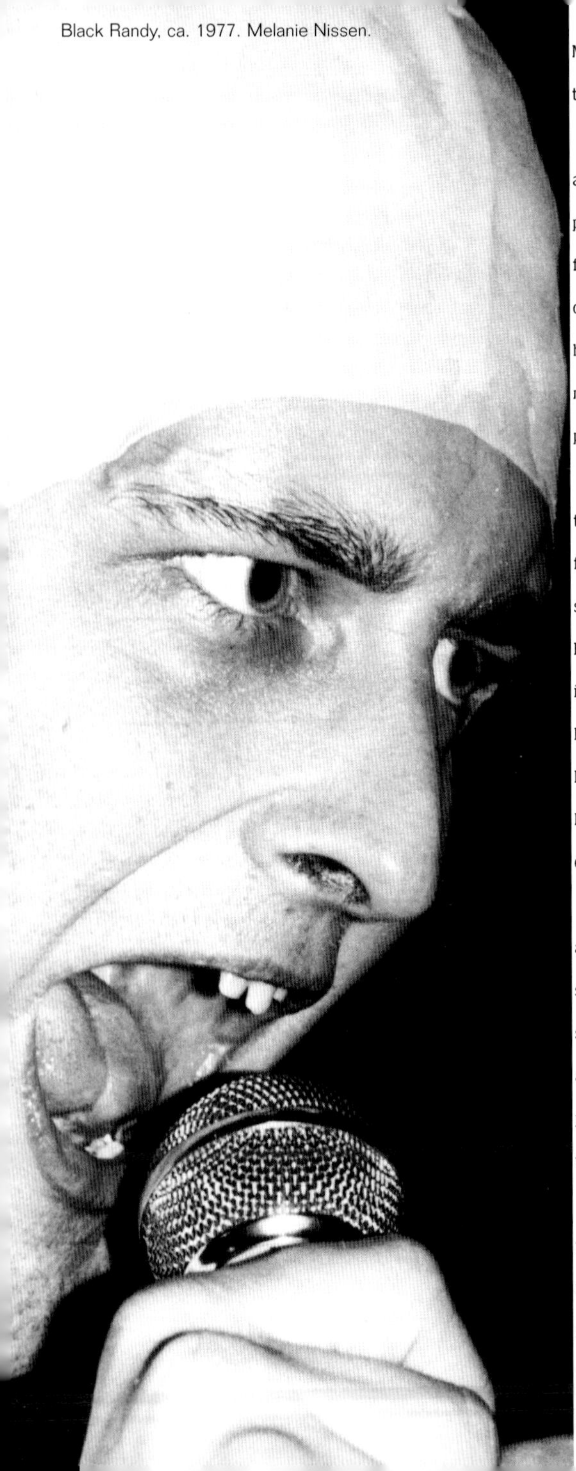

Black Randy, ca. 1977. Melanie Nissen.

Malcolm McLaren, who applied Situationist strategies in his management of the Sex Pistols.

Things were a bit less high-minded in New York, where the punk aesthetic synthesized stylistic motifs handed down from Warhol's Factory, pulp fiction, B movies, and comic books. (New York's *Punk* magazine was, in fact, structured exactly like a comic book.) There were, of course, a smattering of austere art bands—Television, Talking Heads—but Blondie, the Ramones, and the Dead Boys were more representative of first-generation New York punk.

L.A. was entirely different in terms of the diverse styles that coexisted here. With a handful of significant exceptions, however, all those styles shared a quality of studied amateurishness. Fetid petri dish that it was, the L.A. punk scene did include a handful of participants who went on to have significant careers in the arts—Gary Panter, Matt Groening, Georganne Deen, Lou Beach, and Raymond Pettibon, among others—but they are exceptions to the rule.

The Screamers, ca. 1977. Melanie Nissen.

For the most part, the posters, flyers, announcements, and record sleeves on view here have all the craft of a hastily scribbled note left on the kitchen table by someone running out on an errand. In short, a lot of this stuff is just plain sloppy and is a far cry from anything the average citizen would tenderly remove from a phone pole and carry home to press in a memory book. (It takes rare geniuses like John Roecker to preserve these fragile histories.)

Punk graphics of the mid-seventies were hit-and-run because things were moving fast then and it was all about getting information across. Shows were organized, promoted, and presented in a matter of days, last-minute fund-raisers staged in response to various emergencies (trouble with the law, medical costs, stolen instruments), birthday bashes, record-release parties—all were conceived and brought to fruition quickly and on minimal funds. Available cash was usually spent on beer, and people weren't thinking about posterity when they set out to advertise whatever it was they were up to.

Art was a means to an end for them, pure and simple. Some punks might've had a passing familiarity with surrealism or pop art (it's hard to say, because nobody

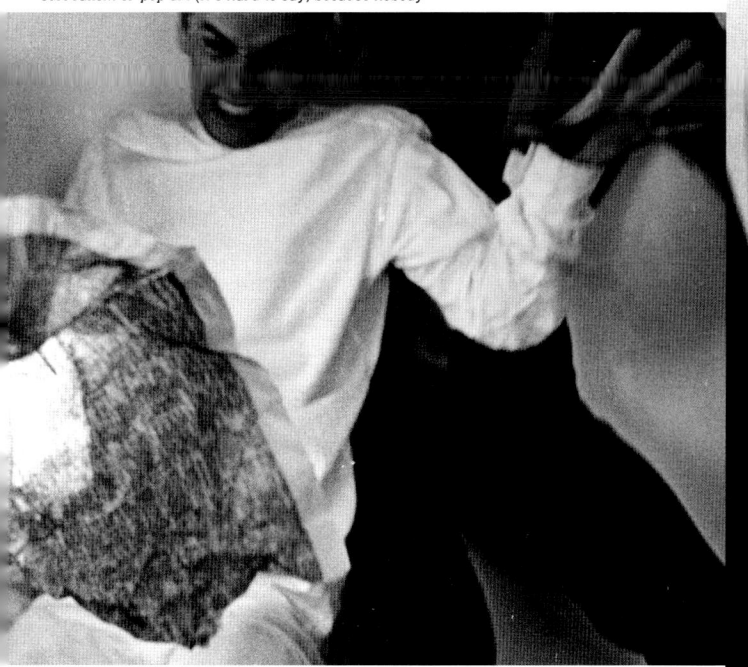

bragged about book learnin' in those days), but it's for sure nobody gave a rat's ass about minimalism or conceptualism, which were the ranking high-art styles of the day.

In classic dada tradition, punks rejected the Academy and drew instead from "low" sources: graffiti, underground comics, advertising, car culture, the tarot, blaxploitation, bondage and pornography, surf culture, fifties industrial films, *Mad* magazine, and the universe of American detritus that winds up in thrift stores. It all got tossed in the blender, and though the results were often visually crude, they were invariably witty.

Tomata Du Plenty (Screamers), ca. 1977. Melanie Nissen.

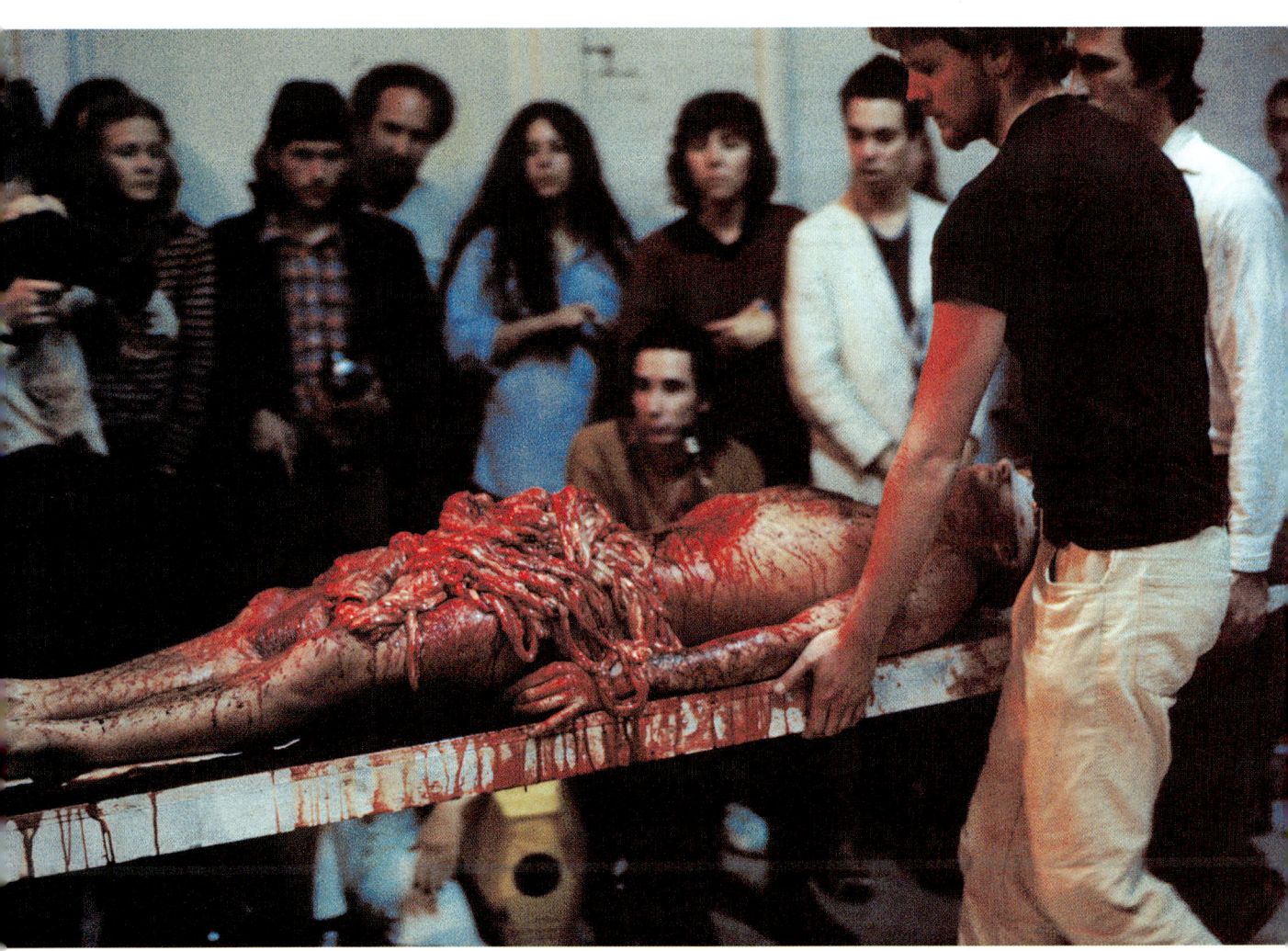

Mike Kelley watches Hermann Nitsch's blood-and-guts performance art, April 8, 1978. Jonathan Louie.

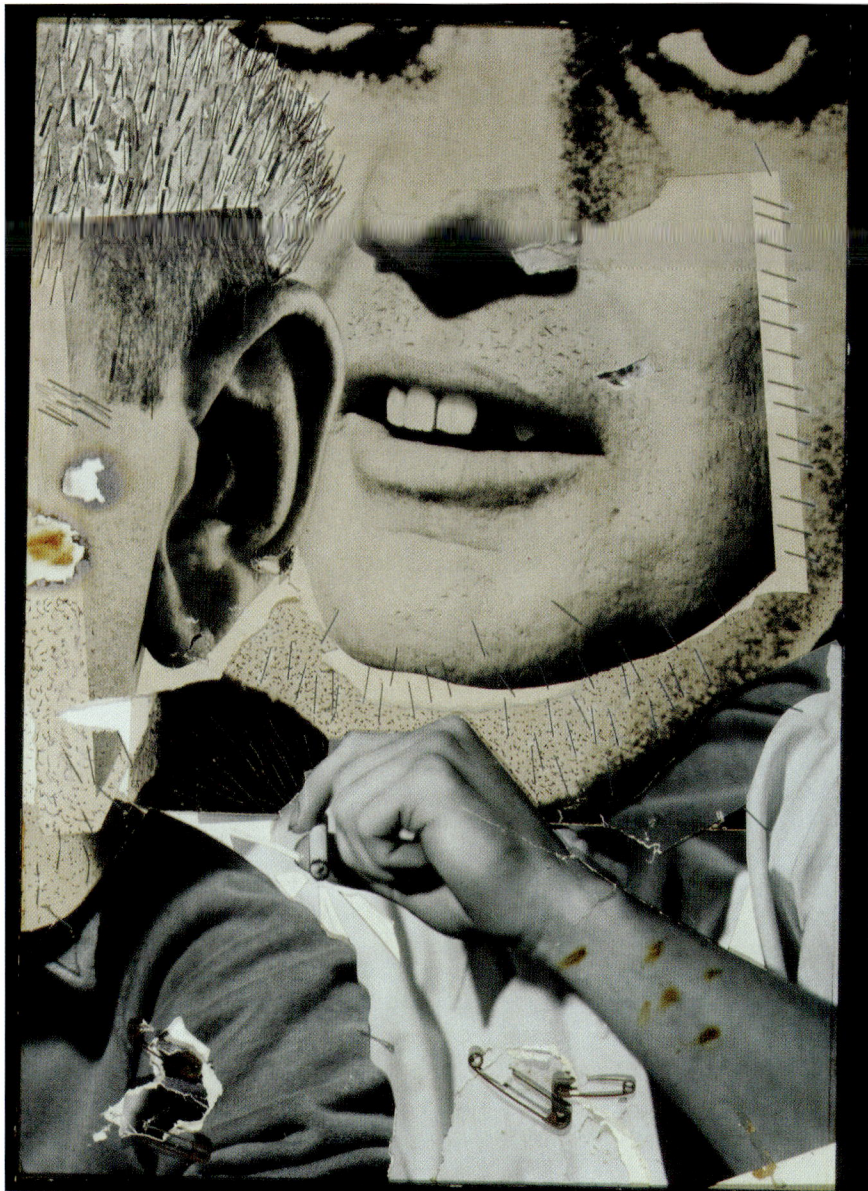
Lou Beach, untitled collage, ca. 1977 (appeared in *Slash*, 1977). Collection of the artist.

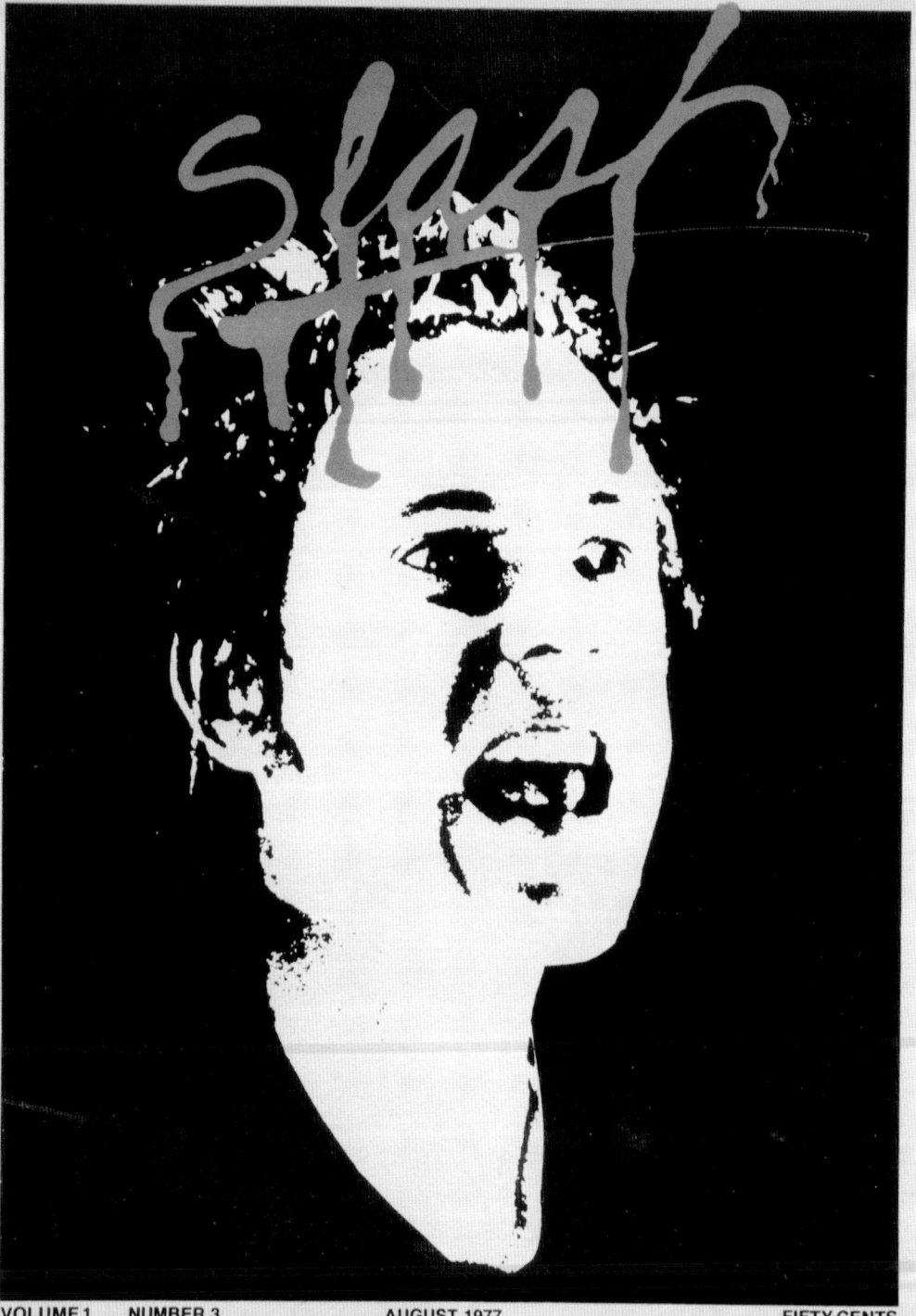

Not enough has been made, in fact, of how funny L.A.'s first-generation punks were. Many of them—Black Randy, Arthur J. & the Gold Cups, the Dickies, Spazz Attack—initially got involved purely as a goof and weren't the least bit uncomfortable making fools of themselves. At that point L.A.'s punk community had yet to be co-opted by the record business and the stakes were still relatively low, so a climate of freedom prevailed which fostered the emergence of some truly original voices.

Exene Cervenka, for instance, developed a visual sensibility revolving around the calligraphic line. Transforming simple journals into illuminated manuscripts, Cervenka's visual tapestries interweave beautifully rendered text, illustrations, and scraps of ephemera—fragments

Slash, 1977.
Collection of John Roecker.

of fundamentalist religious propaganda, personal mementos, the iconography of the Catholic church. Functioning simultaneously as prayer books and as a visual form of record-keeping, her work has a chaotic density that gives off an intense emotional charge.

The Screamers, too, were relatively at home in the realm of visual art. A short-lived group whose mythical stature has something to do with the fact that they rarely performed and never made a record, the Screamers were essentially a highly stylized homage to Berlin, Germany, during the years of the Weimar Republic. A playpen for sexual experimentation which lasted from 1919 to 1933, Weimar Berlin was evoked by the Screamers through the use of German expressionist lighting and chiaroscuro, lead singer Tomata Du Plenty's grotesquely contorted performing style, and the sexual ambiguity of the band members. Their shows tended to be short, fast sets of short, fast songs about bondage and shock therapy which went by in a flash.

The Screamers created very little product during their brief tenure as a band, but lead singer Du Plenty has maintained a practice as a painter independent of his work in music. Du Plenty's fluid, vaguely erotic paintings are very much in synch with the Screamers' music in that they reflect the influence of Egon Schiele, the seminal German expressionist who succumbed in 1918 to the influenza epidemic then sweeping across Europe.

Promoting a decidedly rougher aesthetic were Fear and the Mentors. Like amphetamine-crazed bikers who had somehow wandered into the wrong party, Fear and the Mentors evoked a maelstrom of glistening muscles, black leather, violence, and aggression. At once ridiculous and threatening, their promotional graphics revolved around explosive haiku of profanity and insult.

The Weirdos' gestalt was nearly as turbulent, but much more refined. For instance, the image on the cover of their first single, "We Got the Neutron Bomb"—which juxtaposes a nuclear power plant with a crashing plane—looks exactly like a collage by Bruce Conner, a critically acclaimed Bay Area artist whose body of work includes a series of revered underground films made in the fifties and sixties. Pieced together by recutting old industrial films, Conner's movies give off a peculiar perfume of paranoia very much in synch with the Orwellian nightmare Devo was then attempting to conjure. (Conner, in fact, made a promotional video for a Devo single.)

Slash magazine was the publication of record in the early years of L.A. punk. Launched in 1977 by Melanie Nissen, Philomena, Claude Bessy, and Steve Samiof, *Slash* had a distinctive look that was largely shaped by Samiof, an all-purpose idea man who rarely put his name on anything but contributed a lot. Samiof had the instincts of a firstrate adman and a flair for visual shorthand; his ingenious logo for *Slash*, for instance, is the magazine's title configured as a bleeding wound.

Artist Lou Beach, whose work is often featured in the *New York Times*, drew from unusually pedigreed sources. Beach's collages, which were regularly seen in *Slash*, were squarely in the tradition of Hannah Hoch, a pioneering collagist who was the sole female member of the Berlin dada circle. As is true of Hoch's work, Beach's playfully menacing collages pivot on violent shifts in scale and jarring combinations of imagery.

Gary Panter's punk-era comic strip *Jimbo* also appeared monthly in *Slash*. Chronicling the misadventures of a clueless, forlorn punk who gets everything wrong, *Jimbo* twitched with an antisocial, hallucinatory anxiety that came to be one of the hallmarks of Panter's style. Panter is now a contributing artist at the *New Yorker*, and that he's managed to get his iconoclastic work that far into the mainstream is remarkable.

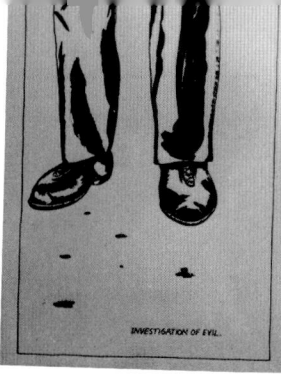

Surprisingly, the work of Raymond Pettibon—an artist who first appeared on the scene providing graphics for pioneering hardcore band Black Flag—has made the greatest inroads into the avant-garde; his grisly adult cartoons are now included in permanent collections of major museums around the world. Pettibon has remained true to his punk roots, though, and has stubbornly refused to become overly concerned with craft. His work still isn't much to look at; rather, it derives its strength from Pettibon's insights into culture and human nature, which are often brilliant and always brutal.

The punk community's belief in destruction as a creative act was evident in its support of oddballs like the Kipper Kids and Johanna Went, performers whose visceral routines operated somewhere between primal therapy and avant-garde art. The punk community also turned out in force for one of the masters of blood-and-guts performance art, Hermann Nitsch, a notorious German artist who came to Southern California in 1978 at the invitation of Some Serious Business. SSB was a production company formed by Susan Martin, Elizabeth Freeman, and Nancy Drew for the presentation of extreme art events; Nitsch's exercise in aesthetic terrorism—it involved dead animals, buckets of blood, and nude young men wearing blindfolds—filled the bill.

Frank Gargani, Ed Colver, David Arnoff, and Kerry Colonna were all making photographs during their punk years, but for some reason most of the significant punk photographers were women. With Melanie Nissen, Donna Santisi, Philomena, Diane Gamboa, Jenny Lens, Suzan Carson, and Ann Summa leading the charge, women dove into the mosh pit and came back with pictures. Needless to say, the odds were against any of them developing a recognizable "style"; photographic style in that time and place came down to surviving the melee without having your camera broken.

Then, as suddenly as it had begun, it was over. The energy had all been spent, some people died, others got rich, colleagues parted ways and scattered to the winds, ideals became confused, people forgot why they'd showed up in the first place. The revolution went elsewhere, leaving us with these souvenirs and pictures at an exhibition.

Raymond Pettibon, ca. 1980. Edward Colver.

At the eastern edge of downtown Los Angeles, beyond the converted factories and gleaming spires of Little Tokyo, lies the Los Angeles River. Like a moat surrounding an ancient city, the river separates Los Angeles from East L.A., the largely misunderstood, ill-portrayed, seldom-experienced Latino subsection of Los Angeles. Although Los Angeles has always been a sprawling metropolis, it may be observed that the sprawl seems to stop dead at the river. Unlike San Francisco, where the Mission district is a thriving and integral part of the city, East L.A. is a no-man's land where few but the inhabitants ever venture.

In 1976, however, the music knew no bounds. Punk arrived in East L.A. like the invention of television—simultaneously and in different places, and like television, it hit big. Everyone claims to have been the "first" person in East L.A. to purchase a punk record: some claims even predate the release of the records in question. It matters little now. What matters is that when the L.A. punk scene was born, Latinos were integrally involved, and throughout its lifespan the contributions of Ron Reyes and Dez Cadena of Black Flag, Dave Drive of the Gears, Gerardo Velazquez of Nervous Gender; Joe Ramirez of the Eyes as well as the Brat, the Odd Squad, the Rents, and the Girl Scouts, among others, were an undeniable part of its history and growth.

EAST TO EDEN BY SEAN CARRILLO

One of the first groups to gain prominence—the Bags—had a magnetic lead singer from E.L.A. Alice Bag, aka Alice Armendariz, boisterously broke free from previously held

The Zeros, ca. 1977. Melanie Nissen.

stereotypes of females as male accessory or pop coquette. Alice neither mimicked nor played to male rock attitudes. Other groups, like the Zeros, were not from Los Angeles, but they played so frequently here that one might never have known they weren't locals. Robert Lopez (now El Vez) recalls how he used to drive two-and-a-half-hours each way from Chula Vista, California, to play shows in Hollywood at clubs like the Masque, the Whisky, and the Starwood.

The Plugz—Tito Larriva, Chalo Quintana, and Barry McBride—was a tight, fast trio whose rendition of "La Bamba" is unequalled. Tito deftly turned the Mexican standard into a freestyle, raging battle cry of youthful exuberance. There have been many versions of "La Bamba"—including one by the Mormon Tabernacle Choir (!)—but nothing beats the unforgettable sight of several hundred people frenetically dancing as if possessed while Tito insisted, "Yo no soy capitalista! Soy anarquista!"

In 1979 Madame Wong's and the Hong Kong Cafe, two restaurants located in the heart of Chinatown in downtown Los Angeles, began showcasing punk bands, heralding an unprecedented reversal of prevailing cultural attitudes. Now punk fans from all over the city were pouring into the backyard of Los Angeles and East L.A.

If punk music had a headquarters it was surely the tiny coffee shop at the corner of First Street and Alameda in Little Tokyo known as the Atomic Cafe. "Atomic Nancy" Matoba—a singer with the group Hiroshima and punk fan extraordinaire—wallpapered her parents' coffee shop with punk posters from the floor to the ceiling, literally. The centerpiece of the cafe was its wonderful jukebox showcasing the most extraordinary collection of punk 45s ever assembled. The Atomic Cafe soon became a punk mecca; visiting dignitaries included Blondie, the Ramones, and Iggy Pop.

Simultaneously, the downtown loft scene was nearing its peak, and the entire inner city exploded with activity and events. Los Angeles Contemporary Exhibitions (LACE) was located downtown in a predominantly commercial Latino area. The Los Angeles Institute of Contemporary Art (LAICA) was on Traction Avenue across the street from Al's Bar and the recently opened American Hotel.

Perhaps nothing captured the spirit of that time better than the monumental Dreva/Gronk art exhibition opening at LACE. Gronk, founder of ASCO and muralist from East L.A., had been corresponding with Jerry Dreva of Milwaukee, Wisconsin. Dreva was a conceptual artist and member of Les Petits Bon Bons; he also participated in the mail-art movement. In 1978 LACE mounted an exhibition of their correspondence and other artworks. The Bags played a chaotic set, and the space was crowded beyond its capacity. Inevitably, the police were called to disperse the crowds, and much of the artwork was destroyed in the frenzy.

The Plugz, ca. 1982. Ann Summa.

The Odd Squad, ca. 1979. Diane Gamboa.

In 1980, Self-Help Graphics, a local arts organization on Brooklyn Avenue in East L.A., became the site of the Vex, a twice-monthly punk-rock club founded by Willie Herrón of Los Illegals and entrepreneur Joe Suquett. This entirely new and foreign concept—hosting a club for one evening at a venue known for other purposes—was an instant success, and Willie and Joe soon had trouble not exceeding the legal capacity of four hundred at Self-Help Graphics' hall. A debt of gratitude is owed to the late Sister Karen Boccalero, director of Self-Help, for her many inspired collaborations that served the needs of the community—even East L.A. punks.

With the opening of the Vex the scene had come full circle. Now Latino bands were playing Hollywood clubs while Hollywood bands were playing East L.A., and everywhere the musicians went the fans followed. The punk scene had done the impossible. It had accomplished what few cultural movements before it had been able to do: it attracted people from all over town to see Latino bands, and it brought musicians from all over the city to a location deep in the heart of East L.A.. The Vex lasted several years in two or three locations. The effortless intermingling of cultures found there has never been duplicated.

Unfortunately, few of the East L.A. bands were captured on tape, either live or in the studio. Except for Los Illegals, who released two records on A&M, and Los Lobos (who were not punk though concurrent), none of these bands were signed. In spite of these groups' tremendous popularity, major record labels maintained a "hands-off" policy—whether due to institutional racism or simple ignorance—almost totally ignoring English-speaking Latinos.

Only Tito Larriva of the Plugz made a dent in this dearth of recordings. Together with artist Richard Duardo and financier Yolanda Comparran Ferrer he founded Fatima Records and released an album by the Plugz, an EP by the Brat, and an album by Paul Reubens (aka Pee-Wee Herman). The contributions of Latinos to the L.A. punk scene may be best known to those who listen to early Black Flag and viewers of *The Decline of Western Civilization Part I*, the film by Penelope Spheeris which includes a brilliant performance by the Bags.

As long as ethnic diversity is considered a "problem" instead of a solution, there is little hope that governments or institutions can accomplish what artistic freedom is able to pioneer. The inclusiveness of the seminal L.A. punk scene demonstrates that alienation and separateness are imaginary hurdles in the face of genuine collaboration.

Fear poster by Richard Duardo, ca. 1979.

The Germs, ca. 1979. Melanie Nissen.

TIMELINE by JOHN ROECKER & Sherri Schottlaender

1976

Glam is officially dead with the closing of Rodney Bingenheimer's club the English Disco and punk is born when Rodney becomes a DJ for the very small radio station KROQ. Rodney, the eternal teenager, plays for the first time in Los Angeles the Ramones, Sex Pistols, and Blondie for the few and devoted.

North and South Viet Nam are reunified after more than two decades; Hanoi is made the c a p i t a l

KROQ opens up a club called the Cabaret, giving new bands like the Motels, the Dogs, the Nerves, Berlin Brats, the Zippers, the Runaways, New Order, and the Pop a venue to p l a y .

Earth Shoes are wildly popular: they are spotted on such icons of chic as Mark Spitz and Tony Curtis

Lasers are used in a rock show for the first

time by the Who

The Ramones make their Los Angeles debut.

Happy Days attracts nearly half of the television viewing audience in its time period; *Charlie's Angels* and *The Bionic Woman* rank numbers two and three in popularity

54.9 percent of U.S. homes have color TV and 15 percent are connected to cable

Patty Hearst is convicted of armed robbery and use of a gun to commit a felony for her part in a bank robbery carried out by members of the Symbionese Liberation Army, who had kidnapped her in 1974

The Nerves book a showcase for themselves and ask the Weirdos to open. The Weirdos steal the show with their bizarre clothes (inside-out pants, paint-splattered clothes) and Ramones-inspired beat. The Weirdos become the first and one of the best punk bands in Los Angeles.

A mysterious disease strikes American Legion

Cherie Currie (Runaways), ca. 1976. Jenny Lens.

The Screamers, ca. 1977. Jenny Lens.

Los Angeles adopts Ohio band Devo, ca. 1977. Jenny Lens.

conventioneers in Philadelphia: twenty-nine die before the cause—bacteria in the building's ventilation system—is determined; the ailment is dubbed Legionnaires' disease

The Germs make their debut at the Orpheum. Known as notorious party crashers who are devoted to Bowie, the Runaways, and Queen, they perform a massive assault of noise (not to mention the red licorice and peanut butter that covered lead singer Bobby Pyn).

Top of the Pops: "Barry Manilow's "I Write the Songs," C. W. McCall's "Convoy," Paul Simon's "Fifty Ways to Leave Your Lover"

Millions of Farrah Fawcett-Majors posters adorn adolescent boys' r o o m s

Studio 54 opens in New York

The Damned, the first English band to tour the States, make their debut at the Starwood in Hollywood.

1977

The Germs become the first Los Angeles punk band to release a single: "Forming," on What? Records.

The Dils' single "I Hate the Rich" is also released on What? Records.

Elvis Presley dies at the age of forty-two

Devo relocates to Los Angeles and makes their debut at Myron's, a downtown ballroom, playing with the Weirdos and the Dils.

Rumours by Fleetwood Mac sells eight million copies: it is on the chart at number one for thirty-one weeks; it is the first album to produce four number one singles; and it remains on the charts for three-and-a-half years

Bomp Records opens, selling punk-rock records from New York and England, and it becomes a vast influence. The store becomes a label and releases singles by the Weirdos and the Zeros.

Red Dye #4—that used in maraschino cherries—is banned by the FDA as a suspected

The Dils, ca. 1977. Donna Santisi.

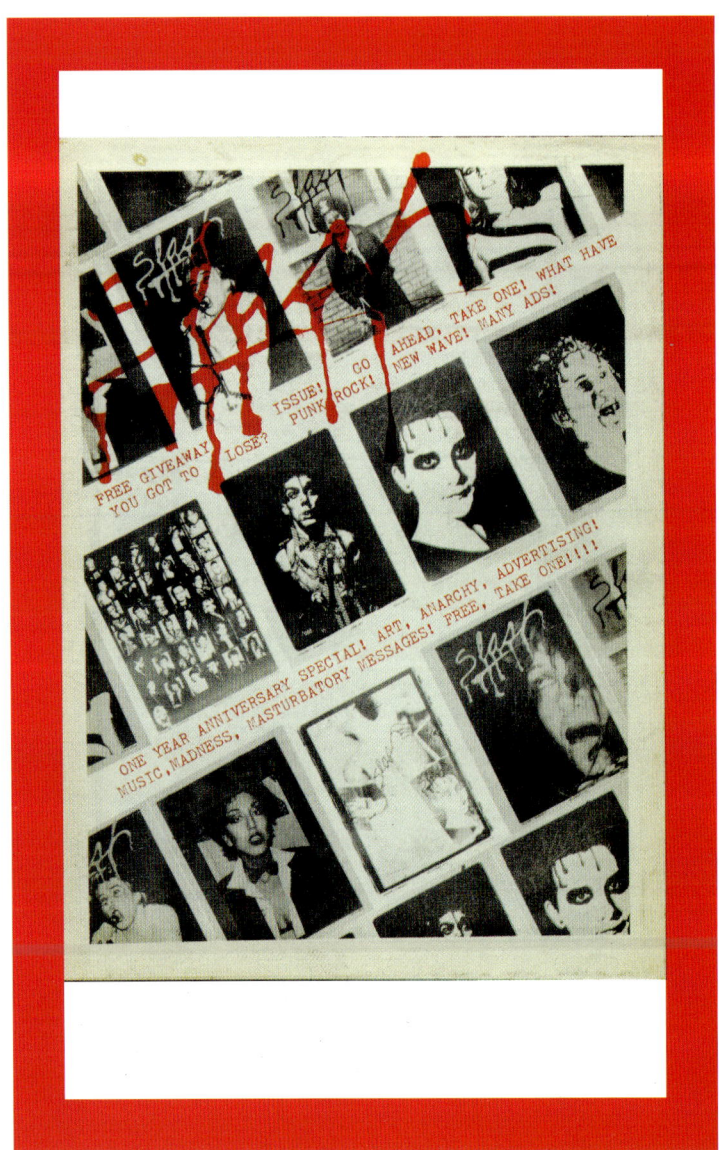

Slash, 1978. Collection of John Roecker.

carcinogen, as is Red Dye #2; the FDA also bans saccharin

Slash magazine hits the streets; created by Steve Samiof, it introduces the world to Claude Bessy, aka Kickboy Face, and the Screamers, who are featured in a large photo spread even though at the time they had not even performed a single show.

Larry Flynt, publisher of *Hustler* magazine, becomes a born-again Christian under the guidance of President Jimmy Carter's sister Ruth Carter Stapleton

X performs their first show at a biker bar in the Valley. Lead singer Exene Cervenka performs wearing a tiara and a pair of boxing gloves.

The Screamers debut at a party for *Slash* magazine; the band is fronted by the hypnotic, spiked-haired Tomata Du Plenty.

Congress votes to raise the minimum wage from $2.30 per hour to $2.65 per hour

Brendan Mullen opens the Masque in a basement off of Hollywood Boulevard. The Controllers are the first to play the club, followed by the Alley Cats and the Skulls. *Slash* describes the club as "the pit's pajamas."

Kim Fowley, manager of the Runaways, books punk rock at the Whisky A Go Go for the first time: the Germs, the Weirdos, and the Dils.

David Soul of *Starsky and Hutch* has three hit songs; other popular singles are Debby Boone's "You Light Up My Life," Bill Conti's "Gonna Fly Now (Theme from *Rocky*)," Rose Royce's "Car Wash"

The Masque is closed when the Bags perform and a drunken Bobby Pyn (now known as Darby Crash) attacks a policeman. The police then proceed to close the club for not having the proper permits.

President Jimmy Carter pardons ten thousand who evaded the draft from 1964 to 1973

The Whisky starts having afternoon shows: the first features Blondie, Devo, and the

The Weirdos usher in a new year, 1978. Collection of John Roecker.

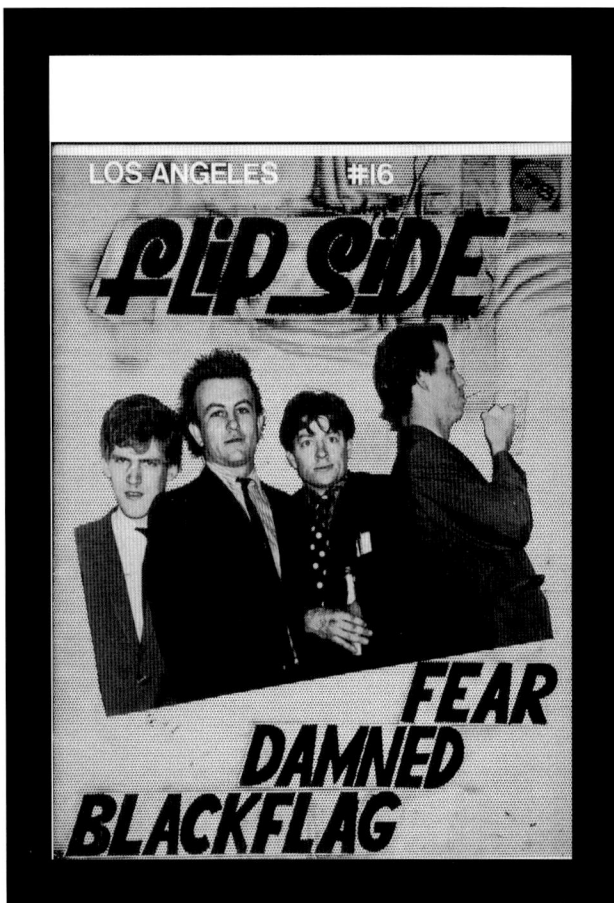

Flipside, 1979. Collection of John Roecker.

Germs, all for three bucks.

The Starwood temporarily bans punk rock when the Screamers burn an American flag during a Fourth of July show.

The Dickies make their debut at the reopened Masque and are quickly dubbed "the punk Monkees."

Dangerhouse Records releases singles by the Randoms, Black Randy, and the Alley Cats.

Flipside magazine from Whittier, California, makes its debut at twenty-five cents a copy.

There are 925 million TV sets in the U.S., 54 percent of the world total; the Soviet Union, with sixty million sets, is second. Americans watch *The Six Million Dollar Man*, *Hawaii Five-O*, and *The Odd Couple*, while the telecast of Alex Haley's *Roots* breaks all viewing records

The Screamers and the Weirdos are at their peak, headlining the Whisky and the Roxy.

New bands include the Flesh Eaters, the Plugz, and the Mau-Maus.

Punk rock makes it to the big time at the Hollywood Palladium: billed as "the Punk-rock fashion show," it featured Blondie, the Weirdos, and Devo.

Louise Brown, the first test-tube baby, is born in England

The Sex Pistols snub Los Angeles, play San Francisco, and then break up. Johnny Rotten appears at the Whisky and meets the locals, including Joan Jett.

Pope Paul VI dies in August of a heart attack and is replaced by John Paul I, who dies thirty-four days later of a heart attack; he is replaced by Pope John Paul II, the first non-Italian pope in four hundred years

Johnny Rotten (PIL) and Joan Jett (Runaways) at the Whisky, ca. 1978. Jenny Lens.

The original Go Go's, ca. 1978. Jenny Lens.

The Cramps relocate to L.A., 1978. Jenny Lens.

The Masque is officially closed down by the Los Angeles police and fire departments.

More than nine hundred members of Jim Jones's People's Temple commit suicide via cyanide-laced grape drink—or are murdered if they resist—in Jonestown, Guyana, after Congressman Leo Ryan and four others are murdered on a nearby airstrip

The Go-Go's, with ex-Germs drummer Dottie Danger, now Belinda Carlisle, make their debut.

The Hillside Strangler terrorizes L.A.: the bodies of nine women are found dumped on Los Angeles–area hillsides. A Glendale auto upholsterer, Angelo Buono, is later convicted; his accomplice and cousin, Kenneth Bianchi, admits to five killings

A benefit for the Masque at the Elks Lodge features every L.A. punk band performing during this two-day event.

A tower constructed of two thousand wooden pallets discarded by the Schlitz Brewery is declared a city landmark—Daniel Van Meter built it in his Sherman Oaks, California, backyard

A&M Records signs the Dickies.

Saturday Night Fever and *Grease*—both starring John Travolta, lately of TV's *Welcome Back, Kotter*—are wildly popular films

Orange County bands rear their ugly heads with the L.A. debut of Middle Class and Rhino 39.

Kojak, The Carol Burnett Show, Maude, and *The Bob Newhart Show* go off the air; the highest-rated shows are *Three's Company, Laverne and Shirley*, and *Happy Days*, with *Mork and Mindy, Taxi, Little House on the Prairie, Charlie's Angels, M*A*S*H, Barney Miller*, and *What's Happenin'* rounding out the top ten

The Cramps relocate to Los Angeles from New York and perform at the Masque 2 on Santa Monica Boulevard.

Masque benefit flyer by Paul Bearer, ca. 1978. Collection of Keith Morris.

NO magazine, ca. 1980. Collection of John Roecker.

You should be dancin': A Taste of Honey's "Boogie Oogie Oogie," the Village People's "YMCA" and "Macho Man" are hits, as are Billy Joel's "Just the Way You Are" and Barbra Streisand and Neil Diamond's "You Don't Bring Me Flowers"

Mickey Mouse celebrates his fiftieth birthday, while Morris the Cat dies at age seventeen

Dangerhouse releases the first X single: "Adult Books"/"We're Desperate."

Physical fitness is trendy: 50 percent of all shoe sales are athletic shoes, and T-shirts—many sporting advertising slogans—become p o p u l a r

Two clubs in Chinatown, Madame Wong's and the Hong Kong Cafe, open their doors to punk rock, and the famous Chinatown wars begin when Madame Wong's bans punk rock after an Alley Cats show: the club begins to cater to friendly bands like the Motels, the Knack, and Oingo Boingo. The Hong Kong still books punk rock, and many fights erupt between the punks and the new wavers.

Anwar Sadat and Menachem Begin sign a peace treaty at the Camp David summit, arranged by President Carter

NO magazine makes its debut.

Slash is taken over by football jock Bob Biggs after Steve Samiof becomes bored with punk.

An accident occurs at the Three Mile Island nuclear plant in Pennsylvania; across America many hairdryers are recalled because they contain high levels of asbestos

The Clash play; the Dils open for them.

Margaret Thatcher is elected, the first female prime minister in England's history

The new Masque opens with a show by the band Levi and the Rockats. Rockabilly enters the punk consciousness, and bondage pants

Flyer by Raymond Pettibon, ca. 1979. Collection of John Roecker.

St. Patrick's Dance flyer by Exene Cerveka, 1979. Collection of D. J. Bonebrake.

Mike (Middle Class) and girlfriend after St. Patrick's Day show, 1979. Ann Summa.

and poodle skirts go hand in hand.

Deaths: The Tinman (Jack Haley), Ethel (Vivian Vance), "America's Sweetheart" (Mary Pickford), as well as John Wayne, Sally Rand (the fan dancer), and Sid Vicious

The store Poseur opens, featuring punk-rock clothes and hair dye; it is immortalized by Red Cross' song "Standing in Front of Poseur."

During the seventies there has been a 281 percent increase in the number of practicing psychologists, and the number of health administrators, real estate agents, and lawyers has also increased; there are, however, far fewer domestic servants, telephone operators, barbers, and tailors

The St. Patrick's Day Massacre at the Elks Lodge: police attack punks as the Go-Go's are performing. Cops swinging clubs and kicking hundreds of kids make the national news as the police blame the kids for trying to start a riot. The media call it the first misuse of police power since the Viet Nam War. After the Elks

Lodge show, punk rock became the number-one target for the police.

Women's wages are calculated to be 60 percent of those of men doing comparable work

New bands Wall of Voodoo, Human Hands, Monitor, Nervous Gender, B People, and the Suburban Lawns bring a new direction to the punk-rock scene: "art rock."

Bob Dylan becomes a born-again Christian

Slamdancing makes its debut with a mixture of Orange County and Hollywood kids hating each other.

TV ratings winners: *Sixty Minutes, Three's Company, Alice, One Day at a Time, The Jeffersons, Eight Is Enough, ChiPs,* and *The Dukes of Hazzard*; at the movies, Viet Nam was a motif (*The Deer Hunter, Apocalypse Now*), as were sensitive divorced men (*Kramer vs. Kramer*) and psycho killers in masks (*Halloween*)

Diane Chai (Alley Cats), ca. 1980. Ann Summa.

Su Tissue, ca. 1980. Ann Summa.

Flyer by Shawn Kerri, 1981.
Collection of John Roecker.

Orange County band scene is in full force with China White, Red Cross, the Crowd, the Descendants, and Vicious Circle (later T.S.O.L.). The single "Out of Vogue" by Orange County's the Middle Class becomes the first hardcore single ever.

On the pop charts: Gloria Gaynor's "I Will Survive," Blondie's "Heart of Glass," Rod Stewart's "Do Ya Think I'm Sexy," The Knack's "My Sharona"

Black Flag releases their first EP, *Nervous Breakdown*.

Huntington Beach scene is at full steam with the start of Posh Boy Records and a new dance called "the Worm." Eddie and the Subtitles' single "American Society" is released.

Slash Records releases *GI* by the Germs, which was produced by the band's idol, Joan Jett of the Runaways.

Keith Morris leaves Black Flag and forms the

Keith Morris (Circle Jerks) with his mother, ca. 1980. Ann Summa.

Circle Jerks; he is replaced by Ron Reyes.

Posh Boy releases the *Beach Blvd.* album featuring the Simpletones, Red Cross, and Rik L. Rik (whose band is stolen from him by Joan Jett).

Jocks go to punk shows and ruin everything for everybody.

More than 315,000 microcomputers are sold, up from 172,000 the previous year

New bands the Adolescents, the Klan, Agent Orange, and Social Distortion emerge.

1980

Darby Crash leaves Los Angeles for London and breaks up the Germs.

Mt. St. Helens erupts in Washington, killing thirty-four people

X's *Los Angeles* is released on Slash Records and becomes (at that time) the

Beach Blvd. advertisement, from *Flipside*, ca. 1979. Collection of John Roecker.

Darby Crash returns from England, ca. 1980. Jenny Lens.

biggest-selling record by any Los Angeles punk band. John Doe and Exene go to Tijauna and get married and then return to L.A. to play three headlining shows at the Whisky. En route to the show, Exene's sister Mary is killed by a hit-and-run driver. The band hears the news before their second show and plays a sold-out show, drunk and in t e a r s .

Ronald Reagan is elected and Republicans gain control of the House of Representatives for the first time since 1956; in Great Britain unemployment reaches 2.5 million (20 percent of the population), the highest rate since 1935 and more than double the rate when Margaret Thatcher took office in 1979

The Starwood becomes the main venue booking punk bands, including Darby Crash's other Darby Crash band. Darby reappears with a mohawk, Indian feathers, and war paint, starting yet another fashion trend in L.A.

Black Flag is banned at every club in L.A./O.C.

Films reveal the zeitgeist: *Raging Bull, Urban*

Cowboy, Dressed to Kill, American Gigolo

Chicano punk becomes big with bands like the Plugz, the Stains, Mad Society, Los Illegals, and the Brat. The club the Vex opens, booking mostly hardcore and Chicano bands.

The "Who Shot J. R.?" episode of TV's wildly popular series *Dallas* tops all records for viewers for a single episode (it was Kristin, his sister-in-law, by the way); it still ranks number two today

Ska hits L.A.: the Two-Tone Tour plays the Whisky with the Selecter, Madness, and the Specials. The Whisky is painted with a checkerboard pattern for the occasion.

Playboy magazine's 1980 Playmate of the Year, Dorothy Stratten, is murdered in Los Angeles by her estranged husband Paul Snider, who then turns the gun on himself; he allegedly was enraged over reports of her affair with *Last Picture Show* director Peter Bogdanovich

Oki Dogs, a greasy restaurant on Santa

Vex flyer, ca. 1980. Collection of Sean Carrillo.

X poster by Richard Duardo, ca. 1981. Collection of the artist.

Monica Boulevard, is the popular hangout and is photographed by Andy Warhol for *Interview* magazine.

Bo Derek popularizes cornrows for white girls after she wears them in the film *10*

On the radio: The Captain and Tenille's "Do That to Me One More Time," Air Supply's "All Out of Love," Queen's "Crazy Little Thing Called Love"

The Go-Go's go on tour in England supporting ska bands the Specials and Madness.

The Reagans' monkey Bob—who often wore a three-piece suit—is kidnapped; he is later recovered safely by the FBI

The Germs play a reunion show at the Starwood: it would be their last.

Rubik's Cube, the Sony Walkman, and designer jeans are all the rage; the first cordless phone debuts, as does CNN, the world's first twenty-four-hour-a-day news network

The Circle Jerks release their record *Group Sex*.

A false rumor circulates that little Mikey, the Life cereal pitchman, has literally exploded after consuming three packets of Pop Rocks candy (washed down with a can of Coke). Production of this popular candy—500 million packets were sold between 1975 and 1980 — ceased

Jan Paul Beahm, aka Bobby Pyn, aka Darby Crash, commits suicide with a lethal injection of heroin.

John Lennon is murdered outside his New York apartment building by Mark David Chapman, a crazy "fan"

The movie *The Decline of Western Civilization*, a documentary about the Los Angeles punk-rock scene, is released. The film includes X, Fear, Black Flag, Catholic Discipline, Circle Jerks, and the now-defunct bands the Germs and the Bags. It has its premiere on Hollywood Boulevard; joining the punks was an army of police in riot gear. The soundtrack is released shortly after on Slash.

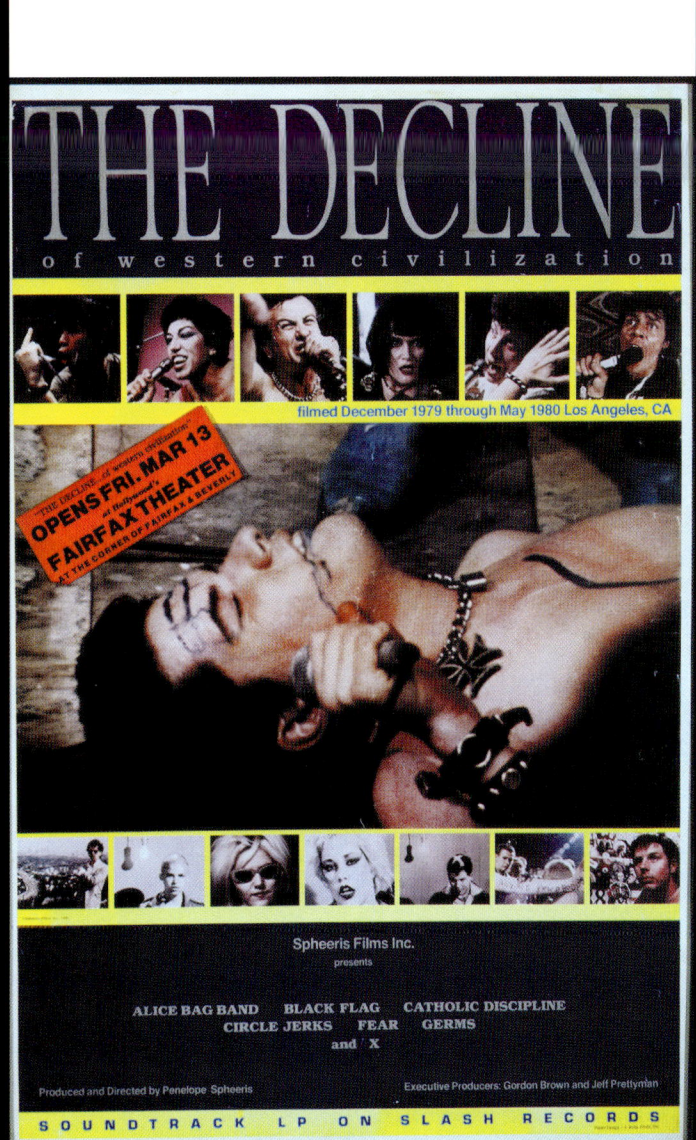

Poster for *The Decline of Western Civilization*, ca. 1981. Collection of John Roecker.

Rozz Williams (Christian Death), ca. 1981. Edward Colver.

1981

MTV begins broadcasting: the first video to air is "Video Killed the Radio Star" by The Buggles

Adam and the Ants make their debut in L.A. and are attacked by Black Flag followers, who will have none of this "new romantic" nonsense. Stickers reading "Black Flag Kills Ants on Contact" are distributed.

Songs on the car radio: Kim Carnes's "Bette Davis Eyes," Sheena Easton's "Morning Train," Diana Ross and Lionel Ritchie's "Endless Love," the Oak Ridge Boys' "Elvira," Olivia Newton-Johns's "Physical"

Horror rock becomes big with bands like Choir Invisible, Christian Death, Castration Squad, and 45 Grave.

Iran frees fifty-two U.S. hostages after 444 days in captivity in Tehran

Roots-rock bands Top Jimmy and the Rhythm

Pigs, the Gun Club, and Phranc play Club 88. Phranc, who was first in Nervous Gender and then Catholic Discipline, is now "just your average lesbian folksinger musician" and makes the punks do the hokey-pokey.

President Reagan and three others are shot by John Hinckley; he is later found not guilty by reason of insanity. Pope John Paul is also the victim of an assassination attempt by a Turkish gunman in Vatican City

Sandra Day O'Connor becomes the first female Supreme Court justice

X plays the Greek Theatre, the first band on an independent label to do so. X has the local band the Plugz open for them. Exene, worrying about the high eight-dollar ticket price, makes songbooks and gives them out to the fans.

England's Prince Charles and Lady Diana Spencer marry: one million spectators line the motorcade route and 700 million worldwide watch on TV

Phranc, ca. 1981. Ann Summa.

X songbook, ca. 1981. Collection of Kristine McKenna.

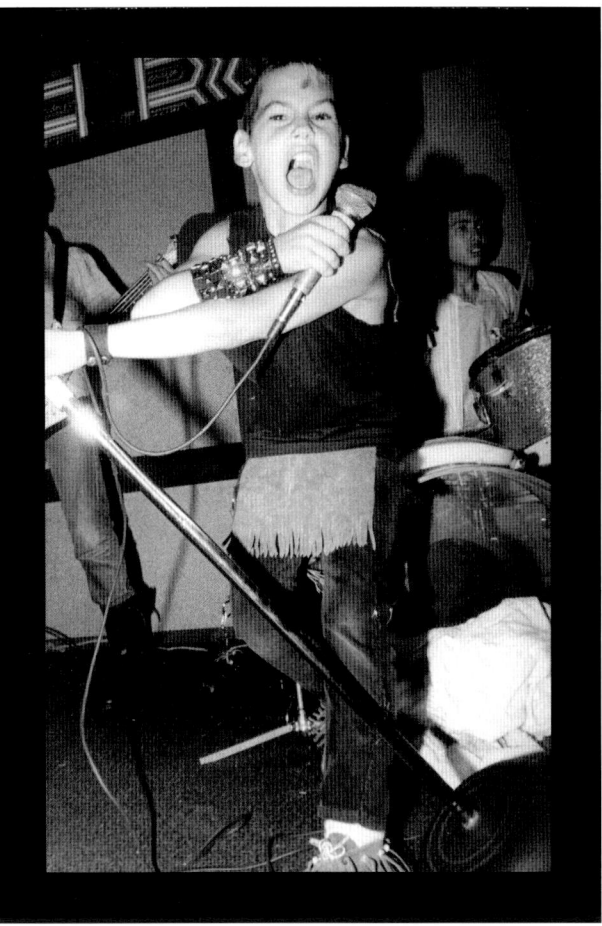

Little Stevie from Mad Society (kiddie punk), ca. 1982. Frank Gargani.

U.S. debt reaches $1 trillion

The Go-Go's release *Beauty and the Beat*. The record goes to number one and sells more than two million.

The Reagan administration attempts to classify ketchup as a vegetable in federally subsidized school lunches

X releases *Wild Gift*.

Firsts: NutraSweet, Donkey Kong, Chrysler's K Cars, the first IBM personal computer, the first Hispanic mayor of a large city (Henry Cisneros, San Antonio)

The Adolescents and T.S.O.L. both release their debut albums.

The largest mall in the world—the West Edmonton Mall, in Canada—opens. It covers 5.2 million square feet and has an amusement park, a miniature golf course, and a 100-meter swimming pool

Argentina seizes the Falkland Islands (administered by Great Britain) in April; Great Britain sends troops; Argentina surrenders in June

Henry Rollins becomes the lead singer of Black Flag.

1982

Science fiction is popular at the box office, as evidenced by *Blade Runner, E.T., Tron*

Acquired Immune Deficiency Syndrome (AIDS) is identified

Downtown clubs like Al's Bar and the Brave Dog house new bands like the Leaving Trains, Fibonaccis, and the Shadow Minstrels. Other bands, like the Bangs (later the Bangles), the Dream Syndicate, and Salvation Army (later the Three O'Clock) are the pioneers of the new psychedelic movement.

Thirty-three-year-old comedian John Belushi is found dead in Bungalow No. 2 at L.A.'s

Flyer by Raymond Pettibon, ca. 1982. Collection of John Roecker.

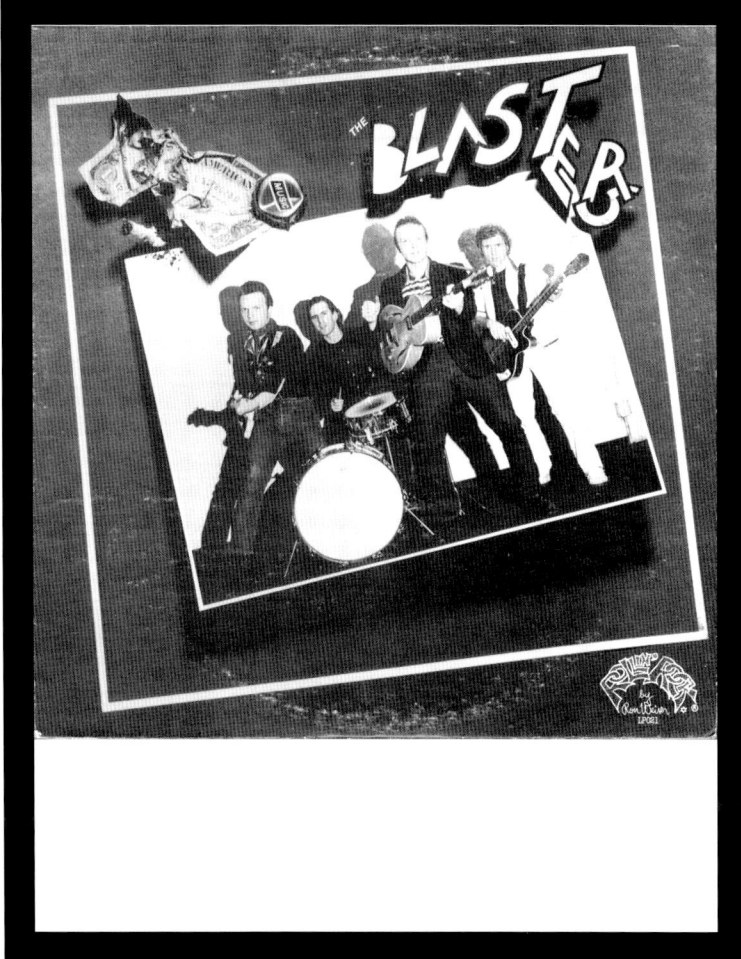

Blasters LP, ca. 1981.

Chateau Marmont; he overdosed on a mixture of cocaine and heroin

Godzillas, a giant punk-rock club, opens in the Valley; Wasted Youth, Ch.3., Circle One, and Youth Gone Mad play.

Architect Maya Lin's Vietnam Veterans Memorial is dedicated in Washington, D.C.

There are 1.5 million computers in U.S. homes, a fivefold increase over the number in 1980

The Blasters become the kings of the rockabilly movement; Los Lobos open for them at the Whisky.

The Equal Rights Amendment fails: it was ratified in thirty-five of the required thirty-eight states; meanwhile, Columbia College, the last all-male Ivy League college, will admit women in 1983

The Masque, the Vex, the Starwood, the Whisky, the Brave Dog, Baces Hall, the Elks Lodge, the Cuckoo's Nest, and the Hong Kong Cafe close their doors to punk rock.

Firsts: *USA Today*, compact discs, Jane Fonda's first aerobics video

A filmmaker, Dave Markey, releases the *Slog Movie* and works on the epic film *Love Dolls Superstar,* his ode to Russ Meyer.

The population of China exceeds one billion

Punk rock dies around this time in Los Angeles and pops up again after Nirvana makes it big in the early nineties and I think they may have mentioned that they like some punk bands and so the media thought that was cool and some bands in San Francisco and in Orange County got really fucking big and started to sell a lot of records and then they bought these big houses and then they felt guilty for selling so much that they sometimes invite me and Exene over to their house so they can stare at her and I can get drunk and pee in the bushes.

Exploited riot, ca. 1982. Edward Colver.

Sources: *American Chronicle: Seven Decades in American Life, 1920–1989* (New York: Crown, 1990); *American Decades 1970–1979*, ed. Victor Bondi (Detroit and Washington, D.C.: Gale Research, Inc., 1986); *American Decades 1980–1989*, ed. Victor Bondi (Detroit and Washington, D.C.: Gale Research, Inc., 1996); Encyclopaedia Britannica Books of the Year, 1977–1983; Jane and Michael Stern, *The Encyclopedia of Popular Culture* (New York: HarperPerennial, 1992); Lois and Alan Gordon, Bernard Grun, *The Timetables of History* (New York: Touchstone, 1979); *A Writer's Companion*, ed. Louis D. Rubin Jr. (New York: HarperPerennial, 1997).

BLACK RANDY & METROSQUAD
STEREO TROUBLE AT THE CUP MO-721

(Dangerhouse Records, 1978)

(Fatima Records, 1981)

(Dangerhouse Records, 1978)

(Dangerhouse Records, 1977)

(Slash Records, 1980)

(Upsetter Records, 1978)

(SST Records, 1981)

(Slash Records, 1979)

MINUTEMEN

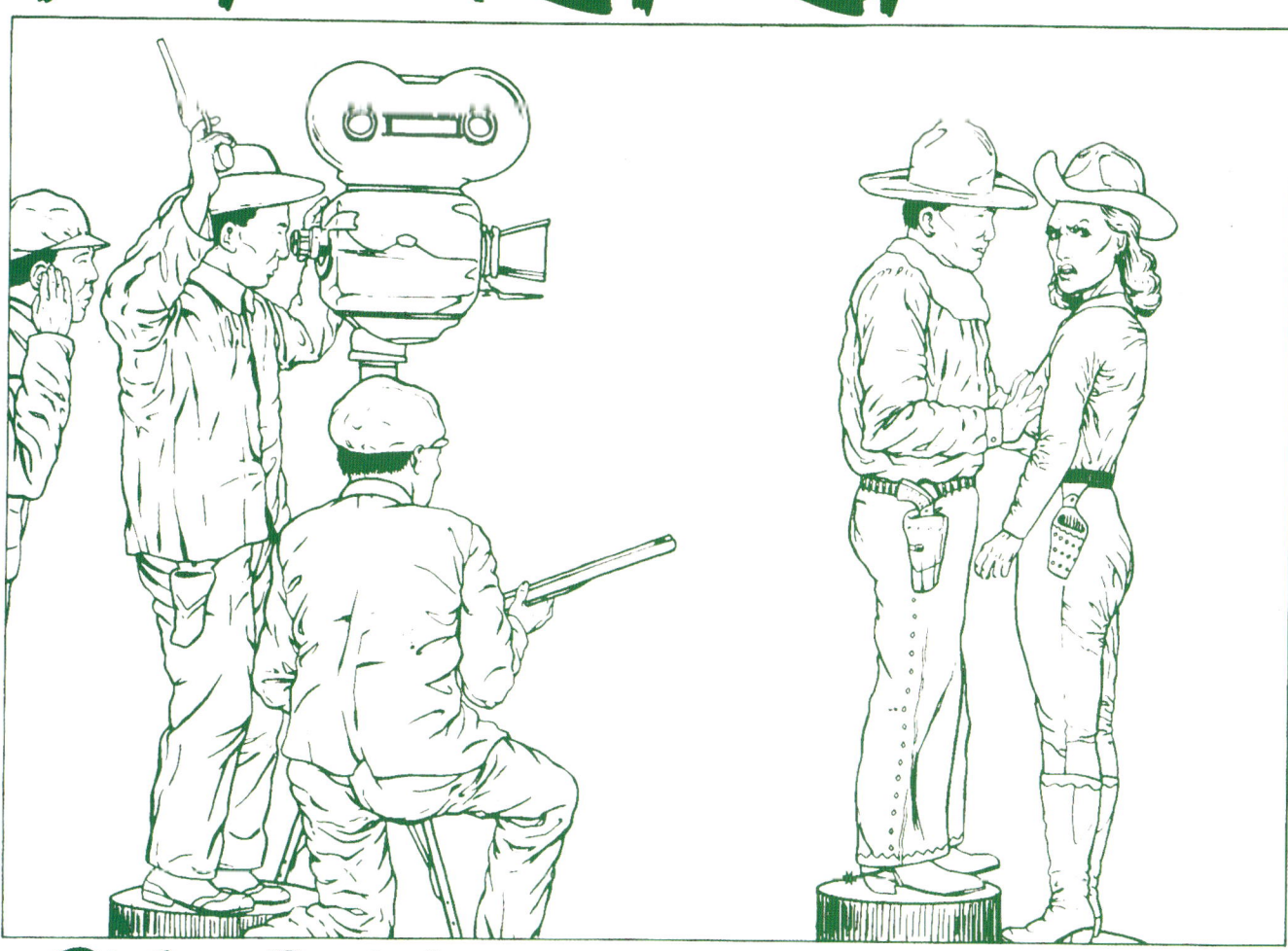

PARANOID TIME

(SST Records 1980)

(Dangerhouse Records, 1978)

(Warner Brothers, 1978)

THE WAY WE WEREN'T

A Conversation with Exene Cervenka and John Doe

John Doe: We were all part of a great experiment. And the thing that bonded us was the music and music as entertainment, music as a cultural reaction, and lyrics as poetry, not necessarily thinking it was "hip," just knowing we were outside of society.

Exene Cervenka: No one was watching. In the beginning, no one was looking for outside approval.

Validation.

Right. Some people had superficial reasons for being in the scene, some people had profound reasons, and some were in the middle.

I gave people the benefit of the doubt.

At the time it was better to pick someone up at the Masque to get laid than to pick somebody up at the mall. It was unbelievable how we all found each other and knew we were supposed to be together outside society, like in Close Encounters of the Third Kind: everybody thought they were crazy, and then they get there and there is a spaceship, like people throwing bottles and yelling "DEVO" at us the whole way.

That's the thing that brought everybody together: "outsider" carried through everyone's psyche. If you couldn't get attention by being loved, then get attention by being bad. We had the opportunity to be outside conventional society and we loved it. We felt totally empowered because there were all these other people validating what we felt—which was "IT ALL SUCKS." Society's not fulfilling, and there must be something more.

So even though punk was nihilistic and railed against everything that had come before—like "kill the hippies," etc.—it was actually a continuation of the freedom of expression of the hippie and beat movements, a rejection of the middle-class values, the hypocrisy, and the commercialism.

The king and queen of the punk prom (Exene and John Doe), ca. 1981. Ann Summa.

It was a bohemian lifestyle. What mattered were ideas and art rather than paying the rent . . . or wearing nice clothes. A lot of people were unaware of how similar beatnik and punk culture were: THEY WERE FIGHTING AGAINST SOMETHING. People tried to enjoy life and live it moment to moment instead of planning ahead and building a future.

It didn't even have anything to do with bands, it was about people being bohemian even though they didn't know what bohemian meant. It was pure, as opposed to Ginsberg wearing khakis in a Gap ad and everyone going out and buying a certain brand of pants 'cause they think its bohemian.

The hippies had anger, but we saw them as kind of running away from things. The punk scene was confrontational; we thought of hippies as weak. The rage we had came from bad parenting and the nothingness of suburbia, and that's also where the lust for life came from. Drinking a lot and staying out late—we really understood that it was HAPPENING AND THAT IT WAS HAPPENING RIGHT THERE.

THE WORLD'S A MESS; IT'S IN MY KISS

No one is united
All things are untied
Perhaps we're boiling over inside
They've been telling lies

Who's been telling lies?
There are no angels
There are devils in many ways
Take it like a man

The world's a mess; it's in my kiss
The world's a mess; it's in my kiss

You can't take it back
Pull it out of the fire
Pull it out
In the bottom of the distance
Pull it out
In chords of red disease
Drag on the system
Drag on my head and body
There are some facts here
Which refuse to escape
I could say it stronger

What was happening?

That the scene was going to be looked back upon with some importance.

Oh, yeah. For about four years the punk-rock scene was so frenzied and self-involved and unaware of the outside world . . . and everybody was so into themselves and what they were doing and what band you were going to see on Tuesday. Or you'd rush off to see the Plugz because you'd heard they had some new songs and they weren't like the old ones—not because they wanted them to sound like the radio or because an A and R guy was going to be at the show—so the songs would be the best and most creative they could write. So we were always running from place to place expecting amazing shows and experiences from each other. It was inspiring and wild. And then, every once in a while, you'd put your head above the crowd long enough to see some outsider taking your picture and think: "Oh, right. This is really important or something." Then it was off to the liquor store and maybe later—for fun—you might attack those same people who took your picture for taking it all too seriously. Or push them and knock them down to let them know that if they really wanted to make the scene, they'd have to pay the price to be there.

Without the *L.A. Times* (i.e., Richard Cromelin and Kristine McKenna) finally paying attention to a club scene that had been missing for so long, it would have died. Eventually we did want attention, but we didn't care about the people who didn't get what we were doing. It was for people in the know, an insular unit feeding off of itself. Every time we went out, I would get inspired—even if it was the Deadbeats doing the theme from *The Munsters*, because they were such good musicians.

People need to hear this again: It was before MTV and college radio as we know it—and punk got no commercial airplay. Only Blondie, the Talking Heads, the Clash, and the Sex Pistols had gotten any kind of exposure in America. Until 1981 there weren't even enough records out to support a late-night radio show. We felt the strength that comes from knowing you are inside something that's bigger and more historic than you are, like the Trojan horse. The L.A. scene suffered in comparison to N.Y. and London because they had engineers and producers who were willing to work with bands. They had Eno, and we had some guys with bellbottoms and long hair who were second engineers on a heavy-metal record—and those were the people who gave us our drum sound, if we were lucky. But there were good people, too, like Geza X.

We made records with Black Randy in a motel room. It didn't matter.

L.A. was never taken as seriously as N.Y.

Everyone believed the media image of L.A.

Laid-back, no problems, swimming pools.

Our recordings were better in some ways because they captured this moment.

It wasn't commercial. Maybe, after all, it was more avant-garde than N.Y.

N.Y. had as much variety in bands as L.A.

We were funnier.

What shocked us when we went to N.Y. [in 1978] was how little bands helped each other. We HAD to help each other here because everyone was AGAINST us.

Like the police and the Sunset Strip.

We were a threat. We messed everything up.

Remember when hippies were scary to everybody?

Exene's journal, 1975. Collection of the artist.

Exene's journal, 1982. Collection of the artist.

J Maybe punk's big contribution to mass culture, the national consciousness, was fucked-up hair . . . like hippies' long hair.

Hair for both: all that's left—our legacy to future generations—is hairdos. That's all they keep.

Exene's journal, 1978–80. Collection of the artist.

Jeffrey Lee Pierce (Gun Club), 1981. Gary Leonard.

Chuck Baron · Jules Bates · Bobbi Brat · Suzan Carson · Murielle Cervenka · Darby Crash · Jerry Dreva · Mike Doud · El Duce · Cliff Hanger · Al Hansen · Rick Inveldt · Craig Lee · Sara Lee · Margaret Montgomery · Michelle Myer · Victor Noel · Jeffrey Lee Pierce · Black Randy · Rob Ritter · Gerardo Velasquez · Chuck Wagon · David Wiley · Rozz Williams · Kevin Wood · Paul Zacha

.R.I.P.

Lou Beach
Lou Beach has been an illustrator of magazines, records, and book covers for the last twenty years or so, in addition to pursuing an acting career, credits of which include *Titanic*, *There's Something About Mary*, and *I Know What You Did Last Summer*, as well as some terrific dog-food commercials. He is an amateur hot-air balloonist as well as a champion unicyclist and trick shot. His favorite color isn't, and he was born under that big red Texaco star.

Sean Carrillo
Sean Carrillo was born and raised in East Los Angeles, California. He was a member of the performance-art group ASCO from 1980–84 and operated the Troy Cafe from 1990–95 with his partner Bibbe Hansen. He is a documentary video producer and often crosses the L.A. River in both directions just for fun.

Exene Cervenka
Exene Cervenka—the undisputed queen of punk rock—began her long and lively career in showbiz at the wee age of three, at the Whisky A Go Go in 1978, when she unexpectedly took the stage during a Go Go's performance and tap-danced to the band. The adults on stage and in the audience were taken by the young lass, and that night a star was born. She not only tap-danced into our hearts, she tap-danced into our dreams.

John Doe
John Doe grew up in Baltimore, Maryland, was educated at Antioch College (Baltimore campus), and moved to Venice, California, on Halloween of 1976. He is currently the CEO of two corporations (Universal X Corp. and John Doe Corp.) and is living and raising a family in Lockwood Valley, California.

Richard Duardo
Richard Duardo has been an artist, printmaker, and advocate for the arts in Los Angeles for more than twenty-five years. Coined a second-generation pop artist, Duardo graduated from UCLA in graphic design and has gone on to participate in museum shows around the world as a master printmaker/artist in a National Endowment for the Arts traveling exhibition. He opened a fine-art printing studio in 1980 and has published more than 450 artists. He was named California Arts Commission's Artist of the Year in 1988, and his work appears in many notable collections, including the Los Angeles County Museum of Art.

Diane Gamboa
"The days of wine and rosaries. The other side of the Sixth Street bridge. Disrespected, disconnected, dysfunctional, and down with disco.... The pissed-off attitude was very real, and it had nothing to do with being macho. Some of it came from racism, sexism, classism, or plain-old hormones. With a handheld camera I shot away at the raw energy using existing lighting. I made a pact with myself to keep the images hidden until 1999. I felt a historical viewing would preserve their remarkable rareness."

Frank Gargani
"When I shot my punk photos, they seemed to be old photographs, as though I was looking back through time. Today, it seems like I shot them yesterday. The punk scene was a nonstop wild time in my life. I miss the excitement and the friendships, and I thank God I survived."

Jenny Lens
Jenny Lens, MFA, has been an exhibiting artist and published photographer for more than thirty years. She photographed the international punk scene from 1976 through 1980 and has been consulting, teaching, writing, and working in the fields of digital fine art, illustration, graphics, and Web design for the past eleven years. She's been happily married for sixteen years (and counting).

Gary Leonard
Gary Leonard is a native-born Angeleno who's been photographing Los Angeles for nearly thirty years. He considers his work to be street photography; his subjects range from geography and architecture to politicians, celebrities, street people, punk rockers, and immigrants. His work can be viewed locally in his Los Angeles *New Times* column, "Take My Picture, Gary Leonard," and in a compilation book of the same title. His photographs are also featured in *Make the Music Go Bang*, another book about the L.A. punk scene.

Jonathan Louie
Jonathan Louie is a design director in print and electronic media. The Nitsch performance photographs are a bloody good example of his personal work.

Kristine McKenna
Kristine McKenna is a Los Angeles–based writer whose work as a journalist grew out of her love of L.A.'s early punk scene. She is presently writing a biography of artist Wallace Berman.

Chris Morris
Chris Morris is senior writer at *Billboard*, where he continues to cover independent music in his weekly column "Declarations of Independents." He followed L.A. punk rock in the late seventies and early eighties as the music critic for the now-defunct *Los Angeles Reader* and he is the author of *Beyond and Back: The Story of X* (Last Gasp Press, 1983).

Melanie Nissen
Melanie Nissen was born in Los Angeles. She co-published *Slash* magazine with Steve Samiof in the late seventies and has been a creative director for a record company for twenty years. She still takes photographs and still loves music.

Raymond Pettibon
Raymond Pettibon was the in-house artist for the record label SST and a contributor to numerous other record companies and publications in the late seventies and early eighties. His work has gone on to receive great acclaim in the fine art world and was recently featured in a major retrospective at the Philadelphia Museum of Art. Pettibon currently lives and works in Hermosa Beach, California.

John Roecker
After being arrested for stalking Exene in the late seventies, John Roecker made acoustic albums with fellow bandmates Mark David Chapman and John Hinckley. He is now an actor on the silver screen; his next performance will be as Radu, an alcoholic baseball player who falls in love with Sandra Bullock. He currently resides on the bad part of town with his three cats, Bun-Bun, Baby Doll, and Willy. (Contributor's note: "Don't just file this one under 'Where Are They Now,' but also 'Who Gives a Rat's Ass.'")

Donna Santisi
Donna Santisi is an internationally published photographer who has been exploring the photographic side of the music scene since the early seventies. Her imagery offers privileged glimpses of some of the most influential artists in rock and roll history.

Ann Summa
A background in sociology and extensive travel in diverse parts of the world have given Ann Summa a unique appreciation for the cultural and economic diversity of the people she photographs. In her work she has documented the counterculture of Los Angeles, from piercing artist Ron Athey and his performance troupe to the *santerias* of East L.A., from punk musicians to actors and celebrities. She often focuses on women's issues and was a founding member of the Los Angeles chapter of the Women's Action Coalition (WAC) as well as the Bohemian Women's Political Alliance (BWPA). She currently works as a freelance magazine photographer and teaches editorial photography at Otis College of Art and Design.

SMART ART Press

Beck & Al Hansen: Playing with Matches

Beck & Al Hansen: Playing with Matches is a lavishly illustrated book that examines the relationship and shared approaches to image-making, words, and performance of Grammy-winning musician Beck and his grandfather, Happenings/Fluxus artist Al Hansen. Featuring collages, assemblages, drawings, facsimile texts, and never-before-seen photographs, *Playing with Matches* surveys the myriad sources, shared values, and performative impulses that serve as a bridge between their respective generations. Al Hansen's collages incorporate the artist's love of found objects—Hershey bar wrappers, girlie magazine portraits, cigarette butts, and of course, matches—as the raw materials for his performances and assemblage sculptures. Beck Hansen is best known for his multiplatinum-selling recordings like *Odelay*, which exhibits his junkman's passion for discarded styles and stances. Both artists seek to transform and elevate the base, often-nasty detritus of every-day life into a dynamic aesthetic experience. Essay by Wayne Baerwaldt; interview with Beck by Carlo McCormick.
Softcover. 8 x 10 inches
144 pp
109 color and 42 black-and-white reproductions
ISBN 0-921381-13-1
$24.95
Smart Art Press/Plug In Editions

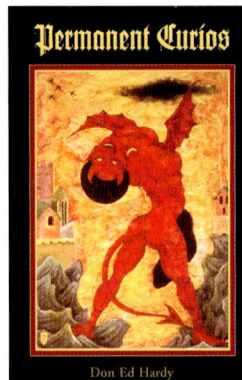

Don Ed Hardy: Permanent Curios

Don Ed Hardy's weirdly beautiful pictorial narratives are drawn from a rich heritage of graphic traditions. Illustrated in this catalogue are a stunning array of paintings, drawings, and watercolors that mine sources as diverse as classical Japanese tattooing, eccentric Chinese and Tibetan pictorial traditions, and the paintings of Renaissance Sienna. Tapping into and twisting the iconography and themes distilled from his twenty-year career as one of the founding fathers of modern tattooing, Hardy's paintings revel in the enigmatic allegories that surround the essential life experiences so often commemorated in tattoos: sex, love, death. Above all, it is his love of drawing—everywhere evident in this topsy-turvy mixing of old and new in subject and technique—from traditional religious iconography and modern cartoon characters to Japanese *ukiyo-e* painting and classic tattoo motifs from World War II which gives Hardy's paintings their raw power, sense of humor, and alluring beauty. Essay by David Levi Strauss.
Softcover, 6 x 9 inches
22 pp
9 color, 4 black-and-white illustrations
ISBN 1-889195-13-8
$10

Manuel Ocampo: Héridas de la Lengua

One of the most important young artists to have emerged from Los Angeles in the last decade, internationally renowned Manuel Ocampo works in the updated tradition of political allegorists like Géricault, Goya, Daumier, and Golub. In this beautifully illustrated book, Ocampo's exuberant works blend high and low culture, academic and popular, the scared and secular, image and text to supercharge canvases with a blatant disregard for stylistic and idiomatic consistency. Gutsy, bold, and filled to the brim with sociopolitical critique and a perverse take on religious themes, Ocampo has perfected the art of the alchemist," transforming horror into exquisite beauty, history into art, purgatory into salvation." Ocampo was awarded the Prix de Rome in 1995 and has been living in Europe for the last year. With essays by Kevin Power and Chon Noriega and a conversation with Daniel J. Martinez.
Softcover, 10 1/2 x 11 inches
80 pp
64 color, 12 black-and-white illustrations
ISBN 1-889195-10-3
$30